THINK OUTSIDE THE BOX

Transform your life by Changing your Perspective

AJAY KUMAR SHARMA

*THIS BOOK IS FOR ANYONE WHO
WANTS TO UNLOCK THE BEST
VERSION OF THEMSELVES AND
ACHIEVE THEIR ASPIRATIONS*

Contents

Preface

Naval Ravikanth once said, "Be the person you want to write the book about". I consider life my biggest teacher and the chapters covered in this book give a glimpse of the traits I have come to develop as I have progressed into different stages of my life. I was sent to boarding school at the age of four and half and since then till today, I have mostly stayed away from my native city, away from parents, relatives, childhood friends and extended family. Initially because of my parents' belief that good education will lay the foundation of a successful career, now to give shape to my career. Been away from family made me physically and emotionally very weak till my teens, which even bothered my parents. I had to work hard on my body, mind, and personality to reach the stage I am at today. Boarding schools made me independent to fight for my needs and wants in a competitive environment. I imbibed a mix of values studying in Uttar Pradesh, Uttarakhand, Rajasthan and finally in Karnataka based on cultural exposure and self-discovery.

I have failed to fulfil my dad's aspirations to become an IIT'ian or crack Indian Administrative services. Life till the time I was preparing for IITs and Post failing to clear the prestigious examination has been like two sides of the coin. From the time of graduation till a couple of years back I was in constant search of doing something to make my dad proud, but somehow, I couldn't do it fully, I felt something somewhere was always a miss, not that my dad criticized me. However, starting the year 2021, I have lived a life on a unique set of principles that I have built with a lot of effort and perseverance. I would be selfish not to share those principles with all of you. They will provide a fresh perspective to look at life, both in good and bad times, and excel in all the four dimensions of physical, mental, emotional and spiritual health. The book aims to provide a framework to succeed at everything you do, if you have the right intent and morality.

As per my experience meeting thousands of people across various disciplines, I have found only a handful of people practicing the principles mentioned in the book, which is a sad state to be. It pains me to see the educational system and institutions are producing more slaves at a faster rate than ever before. Most people are operating in auto-pilot mode and very few people care to stop, look and introspect if they are going in the right direction. Even if the speed is slow but the pursuit is in the right direction, objectives are bound to be met. However, most people go full throttle in multiple directions to make early gains only to realize the waste of time, effort and money. It is unwise. As Humans we are the supreme species born with gifts and talents, however as we age, we get brainwashed by the environment, conditions and conditioning. In times like these the hidden talents need to be uncovered, and it all starts with the way we think, feel, and finally act. Thinking outside the box is not a shortcut to achieving all your goals in the shortest time possible, but it will give you a perspective to channelize your energy in a direction that is meaningful to you, your family, community and society at large.

This book aims to provide guidance on reprogramming the conscious as well as subconscious mind with powerful techniques such as journaling, neurolinguistic programming, meditation and lessons from my personal stories. Another important area that I have touched upon is productivity and time management. Time is a scarce resource, yet the most misused one. My approach to time management will provide an insight that you may not have seen anywhere else.

I tripled my salary, went from not knowing my goal to being passionately driven by the goal, mastering relationships with self and others thereby achieving a balance at both front personally and professionally.

I Hope this book helps you at multiple fronts.

Your transformation awaits!

AJ

Acknowledgments

Over the years my biggest support and critique has been my wife Sanju, this book is the culmination of my curiosity and her persistence to share my experiential learning with the outside world. So, a big thank you to her for being the partner that she is. I would like to thank my parents for their constant support even though I have been away from them for most of my life, being their only son. My mentors Mr. Deepak Sharma, Mr. Sameer Shariff, Mr. Amardeep Adiga, Mr. Manjunath Basavaraju, Mr. R Gopinath, who guided me during my professional journey.

Rajeev Srivastava, Harsh Tongia, Kaladhar Reddy, Balaji Adhimoorthy, Nagaraj Hegde, Abhijit Das, Vikram Choudhary, Ashok kumar Pillai, Ashoo Kumar as peers who with have shared their valuable inputs during one-on-one brainstorming discussions.

I would also like to thank members from my local Community club Ravi Nagappa, Lakshmikanth R, Sharang Gurudutt, Anik Dutta, Brinda Muralikannan, Sayani Bhadra and Rajesh Reddy for their constructive feedback during times of need.

Mr. Prabhakar Reddy for his guidance for the last 14 years since I am in Bangalore. My Close buddies Vishwa, Deepak, Varun for the constant support. My dear sisters Simran, Suman and Manisha for their love.

1. Resilience is a Greater Predictor of Success than any other skill

"Do not judge me by my success; Judge me by how many times I fell down and got back up again."

Nelson Mandela

I survived for the initial 31 years of my life; however, I have been thriving for the last 3 years primarily because of 1 skill, Resilience.

December 2020, I accepted a salary cut of 33 Percent to be able to shift to Lucknow City from Bengaluru since Lucknow was closer to my native place and the possibility of spending time with my dad was too good an opportunity to miss. I would do anything to spend time with my dad since I had been into Boarding schools from early childhood days when I was just 4.5 years of age. Dad was mostly working in Middle East to provide for my expensive schooling and livelihood support to the family for close to 22 years, however Just a year back he had bid adios to middle east to settle back in India. Years of distance coupled with my love for him triggered me to make a choice which not many people would make. Thus, I ended up accepting 33 percent reduction in my base salary without the slightest consideration of how much time it would take to grow back to that base again. I was working for a Health Care Startup based in Bangalore and really loved my Job. This was the same time when COVID-19 was at its peak in India and there was a mass Exodus of people quitting jobs wanting to live closer to their loved ones. My reason to shift base was purely Emotional, lacking any logic whatsoever.

I have always aspired to make a lot of money, more than what my dad makes of course! I wasn't sure how would I achieve my Dream if I shifted to a 2nd Tier City Lucknow. Yet the Choice was made, I gave away most of my household items, couriered what I could and was soon juggling between Lucknow (new work location) and Deoria which was my hometown every week trying to balance both work and family.

Yet! This happiness was very short lived. In approximately about 11 months, I had to shift my base back to Bangalore again. Somehow the rapport I shared while interacting with dad on phone did not transform while we all stayed together in the same house, since both of us had a different point of view to getting things done. Today when I reflect upon, I feel the primary reason for difference in Opinion was that I had been in boarding schools from early childhood (age 4.5) to an young adult (age 24), and began my professional career away from native city in Bangalore as an adult (age 24-30) , I had developed my own unique approach to life and so did my dad away from home for about 22 years in the middle east sparingly visiting India. Both of us took a lot of pride in individual capabilities, dad because he had fared financially better than anybody else in our community and me because I had gone from surviving from an early age to thriving as an adult all alone in different cities without much support from anyone else.

I still respected and looked up to him, yet I felt the way in which we both thought and worked had a lot of differences and the only way I could reconcile the Trust issues was to start afresh away from hometown.

The Reason I share this personal story is, a lot of us take a big decision with all our heart and soon realize the outcome of that decision isn't what we had anticipated it to be. Sometimes we may start a new business with every single penny we have, take on a new job in a distant city, commit to a relationship, buy a new house on loan, adopt a pet, get married, relocate in a new city or anything else. The emotional attachment behind the decision is so huge that failure shakes us up from top to bottom and we are not sure how to recover in this time of emotional crisis.

I had failed at the biggest decision I had taken to Relocate; I was in emotional pain, yet I couldn't complain to anyone. I had just one tool to my defence, my own mindset. Mindset which stemmed from having faith in my abilities to excel no matter what challenges came along the way. This is how I have grown up at most stages in my life, I just know deep down I can get back up and excel eventually whatever I set out to achieve.

Science defines this as Resilience, which is your ability to persist doing what's best for you in the storm of difficulties.

If you have failed at business or job...
If you are unable to provide for your family...
If you have failed at relationships or had a breakup...
If you are struggling to make your ends meet...
If you have been humiliated because of your looks or skill gap...
If you have a mental or physical limitation...

And choose not to Give Up!! YOU ARE RESILIENT. You are Resilient if you can navigate your boat towards the lighthouse no matter the scale of difficulties that come in your way.

As per an Extensive Research by Angela Duckworth[1] an American Psychologist on Salespeople, School students, military professionals, Teachers and many other diverse groups of people she found out one characteristic as a significant predictor of success, and it wasn't good looks, IQ or emotional intelligence. It was GRIT which is passion plus perseverance put together for a very long-term goal.

As a society we are made to believe that if we fail at something, that's the end of the road and nothing more can be done. In fact, if you just changed your mindset and categorized failure as a temporary occurrence you will continue to rise for every consecutive attempt you make. This would develop your "Openness to new Experience" trait as well, which is an important predictor of the type of personality you have.

To change your mindset, understand first about your personality type. Your current Biases, Preconceptions and motivations.

There are 5 Types of Personality also commonly referred to as "The Big 5" developed by several Psychologist like Lewis Goldberg, Paul Costa, Robert McCrae and others to name a few which defines the 5 dimensions of personality as

    i.   Openness (to experience)
   ii.   Conscientiousness
  iii.   Extraversion
  iv.   Agreeableness
   v.   Neuroticism

Openness to experience is about high-risk taking appetite, not following the conventional methods, curiosity to try new things. People high in Openness seek new ways of doing things and do not stick to one routine. They are highly curious and are always trying to experiment and learn new things.

Conscientiousness is about the ability to exercise caution in action, being organized, systematic and disciplined. People high in Conscientiousness are punctual, detail oriented and abide by the rules.

Extraversion is about how outgoing and sociable someone is. People high in extraversion are very energetic and can be easily spotted at social gatherings. They will take the lead in group settings generating energy from the crowd.

Agreeableness is about how compassionate and caring someone is. People high in agreeableness tend to be very warm and welcoming. They are kind and compassionate and try to accommodate other's interest first.

Neuroticism is about how well someone can manage their emotional state. People high in neuroticism tend to get carried away in the current emotional state. They are more prone to anxiety, stress and depression.

These 5 personality types have both upper and lower scales. You must identify what your personality type is to start working on your mindset since your external persona reflects your internal mindset. Thus, it's imperative to bring a transformation externally you must start the work internally.

Some People are naturally Resilient than others, yet resilience is partially hereditary. It is shaped by the environment, Choices and conditioning that you are exposed to. It gets strengthened with every little choice you make on a day-to-day basis. Your actions are based on your deeply held beliefs, some of them you might consciously know but a lot of your beliefs are woven deep into the subconscious that you do not know.

Aristotle said, "Knowing yourself is the beginning of all wisdom", John C maxwell says, "Know yourself to grow yourself"

These 2 words "knowing self" is the most fundamental requirement to "improving self" otherwise we would keep copying what our friends, neighbors, and peers do but our personality, our aspirations, our skillset are contrastingly different than theirs. We cannot have what others are having by doing exactly what they are doing. If our actions are not aligned with our passion the results will always be a distant dream. Even If we achieve success, it will be short lived because we cannot sustain that which we do not love, that which we do not associate with. Internal congruence is far more important than external congruence.

We are talking about "knowing self" because it is an integral part of building Resilience as a skill. It can be acquired with Practice but requires frequent self-reflection.

Here are 3 simple ways to practice Self Reflection:

1) Start journaling, or Diary writing:

Putting down your thoughts on paper reduces the clutter inside your head however when done regularly patterns begin to emerge about the personality. We learn why we do, what we do without going to a psychologist or any mind reader. There has been various research on how journaling reduces stress, Anxiety and depression. In some cases, it has started to show result in as soon as 30 days. Initial Couple of days will be hard but try to sustain the routine for about a month. If you have a moving schedule, try to give yourself 15 mins during the day whenever you can. Some people even prefer voice recordings while they commute back in their cars.

2) Meditate as often as you can:

Give yourself 10 mins first thing you get up in the morning to get your intentions right. This one hack will increase your productivity throughout the day. However, plan to mediate for 5-10 mins 2-3 times during the day as your schedule permits. This will reduce the anxiety, increase the focus and productivity multi-fold. As you meditate do not try to suppress your thoughts instead let them flow with fluidity. We will talk about reframing the negative thoughts positively in the subsequent chapters. If you are new to meditation, just close your eyes and focus on your breaths as you inhale and exhale, and once the body is calm after few breaths, direct your concentration to any topic that you want.

3) Question every action

It is said that if you asked yourself the right questions, you would achieve all your aspirations with great ease. Revisit the decisions that you have made and analyse objectively as a third person if you made the right choice. There are always 3 perspectives to any situation. First is your own perspective, second is the other person's perspective who is affected and third is the neutral observer who is not part of the conversation and is only observing the whole episode. 9/10 times your own perspective would be biased for the choices you have made and so will be the second person's perspective however the third person will provide a point of view which is mostly missed. While you self-reflect consider questioning yourself from the third person's point of view to decide if what you did was the right thing to do or not. There is a very good chance you will change the behaviour for a similar situation in future.

Knowing self is not just being present in the situation, having the memory skills to answer any objection. It is also about knowing the reasons for your biases, actions and inactions. This requires one to stop and think, which is very boring exercise as per today's standard of living. Thinking about the thoughts that transpired our actions in the past and questioning the credibility of that thought now when there is no performance pressure, makes us analyze if that kind of thought should be nurtured or nullified.

Indian History is full of Leaders who persisted long enough to bring about a radical transformation at the societal level. Leaders like Narendra Modi, Ratan Tata, Narayana Murthy, had a vision on which they persisted for years together to make that a reality.

Narendra Modi the current Prime Minister of India, used to sell tea in his early days and today he is the most inspirational leader of the world. He is a perfect example of Hard work and Resilience. His strategies as a chief mister of Gujarat for 12 years brought about an economic transformation in the state across various sectors. His vision was always long-term, from reviving the water crisis in Gujarat when he took office in the year 2001, to provide 24*7 electricity to farmers, to attract billions through vibrant Gujarat summit promoting Gujarat as an investor friendly state. Top leaders of the world today are taking a leaf out his strategic approaches and the passion with which he drove initiatives.

Ratan tata's Relentless pursuit of Excellence during his tenure as chairman from 1991-2012 made Tata a global conglomerate, increasing the market capitalization 17 times by aligning the focus of each of its offerings and strategic acquisitions of brands like Tetley in 2000, Jaguar Land Rover in 2008 amongst others. He made Tata a truly global brand under his astute Leadership.

Narayan Murthy[2] founder of Infosys in his Pre-Commencement address at New York University in 2007 says that after mistakenly took by Bulgarian guards as criticizing the communist government of Bulgaria, he was held in a small 8*8 bitterly cold room without food and water for over 72 hours and had lost the hope of ever seeing the outside world again in the year 1974. Finally, he was let go with a warning on a train to Istanbul (since India was a friendly country) and being hungry for 108 hours he thought to himself that Entrepreneurship resulting in large scale job creation was the only viable mechanism of eradicating poverty in the societies. And finally, he founded Infosys in the year 1981. The sheer perseverance and values with which he has led from the front has made Infosys amongst the Top Global software Consulting companies today.

Such is the story of every other great Leaders as well, filled with Grit and Determination to do what is necessary. A great Leader always values other's interest first over self-interest, with a long-term vision and strategy.

Building Resilience starts with accepting reality as is. Most people begin reacting negatively to failure, forgetting the fact that failure is just a temporary occurrence. Some people get emotionally consumed into Frustration, Disappointment, Shame or Embarrassment.

That is why self-awareness is important. The ability to analyze one's own actions and do what is morally right in every situation. This is one of the toughest skills to master, yet not impossible! There isn't any secret formula as well, all you need is a strong will. Will to improve beats talent eventually. For e.g.: In the court of law the lawyer who wins isn't the one who is better educated but the one who is better prepared, since every new case comes with its own set of intricacies and requires the will to study them at depth. Such is life, a lot of people who achieve materialistic success in terms of a big house and luxurious cars soon become ignorant about their own mental state of being. They let emotions dictate their actions unsure how these actions are affecting their own well-being leading to a situation of downfall.

Being aware of your emotional state allows you to put a tap on it. If someone made you angry, can you hold your response for just 10 seconds before you replied? Just by delaying your response you are letting your thoughts become clearer.

Whenever you feel emotionally charged in the moment, count backwards from 10 to 1 and categorize the emotional state you are in. If are you feeling angry, ask yourself what is the implication of the action that you are about to take on yourself and the other person, is this the best response you have, will you be able to continue talking to the person after your response, will you share the same rapport, can you analyze the problem objectively without thinking of the person who has said it. Sometimes just by associating the problem with the person we make it bigger than it is. For example: if someone lower in hierarchy says in a joint meeting that you are not doing your job well? Here, since it is said by a junior it is more offensive or does the statement really hold weight, that you indeed are not living up to the standards?

Count backwards from 10 and separate the person and the problem. Address the problem first, the person who has questioned your ability had the courage to face the consequences by highlighting a problem in an open forum. In the process you have become aware of your conduct through someone else's lens which must have come from your own self-awareness by practicing self-reflection. I am not saying that everyone will highlight a situation for the sake of addressing a problem, some will just dig dirt, seek attention and those sets of people need to be handled differently.

At the end of it all its interconnected, self-reflection helps build self-awareness, being aware of your emotional state, you can now choose to do what is beneficial for you in both short term and long term, most people who aren't self-aware are only thinking of the current moment. A lot of your actions also stem from the type of personality you have like Openness, Conscientiousness, Extraversion, Agreeableness, and Neuroticism However by practicing self-reflection with the 3 methods discussed before you can change your personality to align with the long-term vision you have of yourself. And to persist with that vision for the long term is nothing but Resilience.

I have failed more than I have succeeded, yet I have always stood back up again to give it another go, and every time I have made that choice, I have become a better version of myself. It is very difficult to make hard choices, however if you can prime yourself to be friends with adversity, first by accepting it and then by negating it, you will continue to thrive in every endeavor you take.

It took me about 2.5 years to earn back the trust of my dad again while continuing to stay in a distant city in Bangalore. I attribute this to my persistence in doing what was needed and not acting in the heat of the moment impulsively. Today I take a pause before doing anything and only make a commitment when I know I can see through it. Well, this doesn't mean I get everything right, but I am getting better every day with my choices and will continue to improve since I have the resilience to do it.

So can you!

Chapter Summary:

1) Resilience is your ability to persist doing what's best for you in the storm of difficulties. It is a skill which can be built with sufficient practice.
2) Resilience is passion plus perseverance put together. You cannot sustain something which you are not passionate about for a very long time.

3) Knowing self is the most fundamental requirement to improving self, the best way to know self is to practice self-reflection
4) Understand your own personality type. Remember the acronym OCEAN, where O stands for Openness to experience, C stands for Conscientiousness, E for Extraversion, A for agreeableness and N for neuroticism
5) 3 Simple ways to build self-reflection is to start journaling, meditating as frequently as possible even for a few mins, and questioning your every action. Journalling has proven to be a very effective strategy to reduce stress, anxiety and depression. Some studies have shown that journalling starts giving positive results in as fast as 30 days.
6) Failure is a temporary occurrence, treat it as such. This will give you enough motivation to continue trying till success is achieved
7) Count from 10 to 1 whenever you feel emotionally charged. Categorise the emotional state you are feeling in the moment. This will change the way you respond.
8) Separate the problem and the person, this will help you analyse the problem more objectively with less bias that you might have for the person.

2.Reframe Every Situation Positively

"When we are no longer able to change a situation, we are challenged to change ourselves."

Victor Frankl

I missed my train from Gorakhpur Railway Station (the world's largest railway station platform then) when I was 17 years old travelling alone, to go my Boarding school in Dehradun in the year 2007.

Only recently in 2023, Hubballi railway station in Karnataka overtook Gorakhpur as the world's longest railway station at 1507 meters compared to Gorakhpur's 1366 meters.

Coming back to the story, the train that I was supposed to get on was Rapti Sagar which Operated between Gorakhpur city and Dehradun covering 815 kilometres.

Today there are plenty of travel options like fight and buses available across different time zones, however in those times, only direct route of conveyance was through Indian railways.

A 17-year-old travelling without an escort was very uncommon in those days. Today the conveyance has become far safer, and children, pre-teens and teens are comfortably travelling alone to distant cities.

So, what did I do as a teenager then? Well, I was scared to death and called my dad who was in Abu Dhabi, United Arab Emirates from a calling center. In those days mobile phones used to be a rarity and only VVIP's would have one. The more affordable route was a calling center more commonly referred to as STD-ISD-PCO center in those days. I made the ISD call to Abu Dhabi, ISD calling rate was approximately 60-80 Rs per minute and conversations had to be very sharp and so was mine.

Dad, I missed by train was my feeble outcry on the telephone. But dad heard it very clearly in the very first moment and did not shout on me at all but said something that was very harsh for a 17-year-old boy who had missed his train, instead of comforting me or providing a suggestion he just said, "I don't know what you will do" and hung up. And I was in shock, first because I had missed my train and second because dad said he doesn't know what I will do in that moment harshly.

Well, I was frightened! at the same time did not want to disappoint my dad further, I made a mental resolve that I will reach Dehradun by any means possible, and I did so by changing 2 trains in between, travelling in general compartments without tickets, double checking with many co passengers if I was in the right train for the right destination. If You are a millennial and have commuted with Indian railways as a teen even with escorts, you can relate to this much more easily.

Today I understand his reasons for being a little harsh on me at that time, since he was almost spending 50% or more of his earnings on my school education, having admitted me to one of the best schools in India.

I went on to travel alone thereafter without much difficulty, courtesy one incident which gave enough exposure to travelling by public transport alone.

Of course I did not know Positive Re-Framing then, I had resilience as an innate quality coupled with situational awareness that helped me reach the required destination to my boarding school. But I attribute my travel related intelligence to that one episode which has changed the way I plan for long distance travel even today by any means whatsoever.

I am sure sometimes you might have also missed your flight, train or bus. Can you re-visit that moment and think what your response was? Most often it is with filled with Anxiety, Nervousness, frustration and anger.

Similarly, not just at travel, let us look at other avenues of life as well. What is your response when you meet with a setback, how do you look to remedy the situation.

What if you lost a large sum money of money to an investment advice you heard...?
What if you failed at the final chance you had to crack interview of your dream company...?
What if your efforts are not adding to the career progression plan...?
what if you are always sidelined at the time of promotions...?
What if you are discriminated because of your colour and race...?
What if you heard bad news, loosing someone you deeply love...?
What if you fail to live up to the expectations of your parents...?

Everyone has got a unique set of Challenges in life, specific to them. The first and the foremost step to addressing those challenges is to have Resilience, the second is Positive Reframing. If you went to a local priest in the time of sorrow or defeat, he would say, have faith, God is watching, and he will help you at the right time. Look at Building resilience as equivalent to having faith advised by the spiritual Guru. Next step after that is working towards the betterment of the situation by Reframing.

Positive Reframing is like having the stomach of a shark. Sharks can store food inside their stomach for weeks, digest it slowly and their stomach adapts based on the size of the prey.

You must also look at all negative encounters as such. Hear and observe everything in detail, no matter how big the problem, how urgent the matter, take your time to fully comprehend the situation. Only and only then, accept it, digest it and impress upon the memory. Having understood the situation will give you clues on how to mitigate the problem effectively. Mistakes happen when responses are rushed without fully understanding what needs to be done.

At the same time always remember time, money & energy that you give towards a Goal is never wasted. You might not achieve the results you had set out to achieve as planned but it all comes back to you if you continue to have faith in your abilities and stay resilient in your pursuit.

I spent about 5 lakhs and 2 years of effort on a double certification course offered in collaboration from a Top Indian and a UK Based Institute. I did so, in the hope of making big bucks in the field of data science and business analytics since it is an in-demand field. I completed the first half of the course from the Indian institute and received the completion certificate as well but could not convince myself to proceed with the international university. I used to study about 24-30 hours every week outside of work hours but soon my interest faded after 6 months into the course. I do not blame the university! It is just that I realized after spending 5 Lakhs of my hard-earned money that it wasn't the field I am passionate about, and my initial judgement was wrong.

I gave it all, my hard-earned money, my time, and the efforts but it wasn't meant for me to get into the data analytics industry even though it is one of the most in demand fields to be. However, it has proved to be of immense help in finding my purpose, what I really want to do, what makes me happy, what is it that I can do without looking at the clock of the time gone by. If someone had asked me 5 Lakhs 3 years ago as charges to help me find the purpose of my life I may or may not have given it. Yet I am so happy that it has helped me find the real purpose of my life, something I can relate to more passionately. I am indebted to the educational institute for the rest of my life to help discover my purpose indirectly.

This is nothing but Positive Reframing. This is what I have told myself day in and day out. I do not know if my decision to quit the business analytics course was right or wrong, but I do know I am happier making decent money doing something that I love doing. Similarly, I have reframed other encounters of my life as well in a way that is beneficial to myself.

NLP (Neuro-Linguistic Programming) says that it is not the individual encounters that impact us, it is the meaning that we assign to each of those encounters. Because based on the meaning that we have given there will be feeling and based on the feeling there will be a response.

The first and the foremost step is meaning, what is the meaning that you are assigning. This is where positive reframing comes into the picture.

Let us explore a few scenarios to understand and practice positive reframing:

Scenario 1: If you lost your job, the easiest thing would be to blame the management that they did not understand your capabilities, they are self-centred, they do not care for the employees, they want to save money so on and so forth.

Yet what if you reframed it as following: "I know I have been let go from the role I had, I think even after putting my best effort there are some things which wasn't as per the expectation of the management" even though I did good, but I could have done better, there is a scope of improvement. In fact, I know a couple of short courses that can help me become better at the job that I do. I might reach back to the management in a few months and see what they have to say about that.

Now, there is a world of difference in both interpretations. In the first instance you started with the Blame game, holding the Job-provider at fault, having a limited understanding of your capabilities. Whereas in the second instance you started with acceptance. You acknowledge that yes, there is something that could have been done better from your end and have been planned to work on those shortcomings.

I am not sure that if you go back to your previous company with the new skills, they will re-hire you. They may or may not, but it will make them realize that even they could have made a mistake by letting you go and the work ethic that you have demonstrated. At the same time, now you are better qualified than you were before, increasing the chances of success because of fine tuning your skills.

Scenario 2: If your efforts are not contributing to your career growth and have led to stagnancy, the easiest thing would be to blame the boss, culture of the organization. Blame Human resources for the lack of learning and development initiatives, managers not mentoring or not being capable of mentoring etc.

Yet what if you reframed the situation as following: "I know I have been stagnant in my current role, I must enrol myself into leadership courses as soon as possible and cannot be just dependent on the company to facilitate that for me. Today there are abundant resources at a fraction of the cost, I should aim to take advantage of that. Culture isn't just Top Down; I am equally responsible for the kind of culture my organization has, and it can also flow from bottom to top. No situation is permanent, my efforts will show the results."

Here are 3 simple ways to practice Positive Reframing:
1) Categorise every encounter as a Learning Curve:
No matter what the outcome, always remember the outcome teaches you something new, something that you hadn't experienced before. All you need is an Open mind to see it. Every action is bound to bring some result, so before you take on the initiative, do an extended preparation, be mindful of smallest of the nitty-gritties, pros and cons, what if scenarios. However, once you have committed to action, give it your best. Accept the result as is. At the end of the day, you must be convinced that you haven't compromised with your integrity and intent.

2) Accept the Ground Reality:
Accepting failure does not mean you have failed. You have temporarily allowed circumstances to get the better of you. Acknowledging the ground reality and then reframing it in a way that easily supports next level of action is the first step towards overturning the situation. By not accepting the reality you are still thinking from a point of weakness and as you delay the counter-response, you keep losing ground. Most of the time response is associated with action, however first response can also

be to accept the ground reality by reframing the situation positively.

3) Think of a mutually Beneficial outcome:
As we meet with a setback, the first thing we start we consider is, how can we seek revenge with those who have put us into this sorry state or make them small as they have belittled us. However, to win people, we must operate from a paradigm of forgiveness. You must forgive but do not forget their deeds, so you know who you need in your inner circle, who are the people you can count on in an emergency. By forgiving and not expecting anything in return you are winning over your adversaries without letting them spoil your party. Don't do something to others that which you do not want them to do to you. Active listening also plays a crucial role in understanding other person's preferences. Kate Murphy[1] her book "you are not listening" says that people get into a blind rage when they are cut off in between, and this leads to the activation of amygdala. Amygdala activation and listening is inversely proportional to each other. During moments like this we must genuinely try to understand the point of view they are coming from rather than becoming hostile.

Remember the Goal is to practice Positive Reframing as often as Possible. From the time you step out of your home while commuting to meeting different people throughout the day you will get abundant opportunities to reframe each of the encounter.

Let's explore few more scenarios:

a) while driving to work, someone recklessly overtakes you and you have a near accident situation. How do you reframe this positively?

You could reframe as: Well, seems there is an emergency that he needs to attend to urgently

b) while you are sequentially moving in the queue at a buffet restaurant, a new guy jumps the line?

You could reframe as: Seems he has skipped his breakfast for the day, let him feed his hunger.

c) Online ecommerce fails to deliver your order on the promised timeline?

You could reframe as: Never mind, I have another pair of shoes for such an emergency.

d) Someone is playing Loud music in the gym while everyone else has plugged on headphones

You could reframe as: seems like he needs an extra bit of motivation today to move his body

e) Someone is talking on mobile while driving his 2-wheeler

You could reframe as: This was the laughter dose I needed for the day; God, please spare his life for the stupidity.

f) Someone is Talking loudly on the Mobile Phone while your wait for your flight at the Airport lounge?

You could reframe as: Looks like he is deeply lost in the conversation and thus become inconsiderate of the surroundings.

In each of the previous examples, I asked first to reframe the situation positively which is against the conventional way of thinking. You might question, why did I not advise to confront the violators? Well, you can always do that but do not do that as the first resort, do it as a second resort. So, what made you frustrated in the moment has now made you to become considerate, and then objectively assess the situation since you are not confronting the violators immediately you are first reframing the situation positively. Feel free to confront or report the violators if the conduct repeats.

This is a very subtle change that you can consider implementing in your day-to-day lifestyle. Eventually you would realise that you are not provoked by these kinds of incidents like before. If you waste your mental energy dealing with violators whom you cannot bring on to the right track, you should rather preserve your energy and exercise it on more important tasks.

Chapter summary:

1) Positive reframing is about giving positive meaning to each of the encounters. Based on the meaning that you have given there will be feelings and based on those feelings there will be a response.

2) Categorise each encounter as a learning curve irrespective of the outcome. Before you commit to action do a sanity check, however once committed to action accept the outcome as is.

3) Accepting the ground reality and reframing it positively is the first step towards overturning the problematic situation.

4) Think of a mutually beneficial outcome. Don't operate from the mindset of taking revenge, forgive and win over your adversaries. Even if you don't win them over, they will not play spoilsport in the future.

5) Every encounter is an opportunity to train you mind, to think positively first. Over a period, this makes you more harmonious, peaceful and a constructive thinker.

6) You can always confront or report someone for their behaviour, but it must happen after you have tried to remedy the situation with love and compassion.

3. Find your Purpose

"The two most important days in your life are the day you are born and the day you find out why."

Mark Twain

Right after my 12th standard I took the entrance exam for Bansal IIT-JEE Coaching Classes in Kota, Rajasthan. I Wanted to get into the IITs, at least this is what I believed I wanted to do even though it was a decision made by my dad.

I cracked the entrance exam for coaching institute and was amongst the top 100 students all India. Even I was surprised, how did make into top 100 of the best IIT coaching institute in Asia since I had been a mediocre student in studies till 12th Standard. This also meant that I was to be taught by my Mr. Vinod Kumar Bansal Himself, the founder of the Institute.

Mr. Bansal[1] was diagnosed with muscular dystrophy in the year 1974, a genetic disease that causes muscles to gradually weaken and degenerate over time. He used to come in a wheelchair to take sessions. He is someone who not only overcame his disability to rewrite his

Destiny but, in the process, transformed an entire city Kota, in Rajasthan, to be known as the Hub of IIT Coaching bringing an influx of billions of rupees in the city across different sectors. A city which was earlier known for its industries was now known for the Coaching Centres.

Mr. Vinod Bansal Used to teach the top batch of the institute at that time, and I was fortunate enough to be a part of the group but was soon pushed to lower ranked batches after each monthly assessment. The monthly assessment was designed in such a way that with each evaluation, based on the marks obtained, batches were re-shuffled to group students as per their competency level.

I slowly dropped rank from the topmost batch to one of the lowermost batches, courtesy my negative scores. Yes, the score card came in negatives and did not just stop at zero. A copy of the report used to be sent to parents as well on their mobile phones. I must say, scores were demoralising for my dad as well as myself. I struggled to cope up with the daily practice papers (DPPs as it used to be called those days), regular assessments across multiple subjects like Mathematics, Physics and Chemistry.

It is said that getting into IITs in India is tougher than getting into the Harvard's or Cambridges of the world. I was 1 amongst 4,72,000 students who appeared for the examination in the year 2010 fighting for approximately 10,000 seats at 15 IITs, and I failed. That means one had to amongst the top 2% to secure a seat successfully. 14

Years later today, the number of IITs have expanded to 23 with 14,76,557 students appearing for the examination against a total of 17,740 seats. This means you must be amongst the top 1% today to secure a seat successfully.

The Popularity of IITs has unquestionably gone up each year and so have the number of applicants. It wouldn't be false to say that each year more than 80% of the students who fail to secure a seat will feel the void throughout their life. And I am one amongst them.

I Had failed to live up to the expectations of my dad and faced the brutal reality that IITs weren't my cup of tea. My dad did not speak to me for the next couple of days. Afterall he was spending a major portion of his earnings on my education, an amount which nobody had ever spent on their children in our community. Finally, when he did speak it was his trademark response, I don't know what you will do in your life and that was all. Here was a 20-year-old young adult not knowing what to do in his life and with no one to provide guidance it was even more frustrating. I had heard my dad saying this to someone that he wanted to work as a chemist after he retires from middle east. Living in a middle-class family in the north Indian state of Uttar Pradesh, we never had a computer or internet in our homes in those times. I spent next couple of days in internet café finding everything that I could about colleges offering a degree in Pharmaceutical Sciences. Finally, the decision was made after discussion within the family, and I enrolled at MS Ramaiah college in Bangalore for my degree. It was planned that I will help setup a Pharmacy for my dad after graduation. After completing my degree in pharmaceutical science, I had developed an interest in sales and marketing and that was the stream I interviewed to work with Sanofi Aventis a French based multinational company as a medical sales representative from early jan-2015.

I did not find my purpose yet; I was doing something that I liked, which continued for the next couple of years in similar roles until I had a life changing period in the year 2021 working with a CEO named Deepak Sharma at MedLern Pvt Limited a Learning management company which made software for hospitals. Working with him, I unlocked my hidden personality, one which was filled with curiosity & openness to experience new things. He gave me newer tasks frequently which almost took about 3-4 iterations to be finally accepted, yet I did not get frustrated or abandon the work in between. I started learning and upskilling what I did not know. Bought the subscription of LinkedIn Learning, Udemy, Other online resources to complete the deliverables and soon started enjoying the process.

My Curiosity finally led me to book reading, which started with "Winning Habits-on the life examples of Swami Vivekananda" by author RK Sharma, then Biography of JRD Tata, Biography of Narayan Murthy and so on and so forth. As I read more my hunger kept increasing with every new book. Thereafter, having learnt from a large no of mentors I could clearly see the flaws in the education system and in the societies. I realised it is everyone's responsibility to contribute to the betterment of the community in whichever capacity we can. 15th Nov 2022 -I made a written resolve to empower large no of people, do whatever I can to ensure, they become the best version of themselves. This was the purpose which finally resonated with who I was internally, resonating with my deeply held beliefs. I had found my calling and now I wanted others to realise this much faster, find their purpose and get started as early as possible.

Purpose means you're Calling, your motivations, the meaning of your life, the reason for your existence. If you were to die tomorrow what is that thing you would spend your time doing today. What is that thing you are willing to bet your life against. Purpose is the fuel that fires the engine. If you used adulterated oil the engine is going to shut down sooner than later. Same is life, you can do plenty of things and you may also enjoy doing a lot of them. These temporary engagements might even bring you monetary gains or any other achievement that you may have sought. Yet the realisation of the result will not give the satisfaction you crave deeply. Deep craving is only satisfied by doing something you deeply love. I am not talking about satisfying the chocolate cravings here.

Purpose has got nothing to with age. The sense of realisation can happen during any stage of the life. Somebody has found it in their teenage some in adolescence and some in their middle age or their old age. Grandmaster Gukesh D[2] from Chennai, India became the youngest world champion in chess history at the age of 18 years by beating GM Ding lee on 12th December 2024. He did so by shattering the previous record held by GM Gary Kasparov for 22 years. Gukesh started playing chess at the age of 7 and dropped out of school after class 4 to focus on chess. In 2017 his father quit his job as an ENT Surgeon to travel with Gukesh and his mother took the mantle of supporting the family financially. Gukesh identified his purpose early on in his life and his parents supported him whole heartedly. This is how strong purpose is.

Similarly other great leaders have not just transformed themselves but also brought about transformation in the societies by staying committed to their Purpose. Sachin Tendulkar by his commitment to Cricket. He became the highest run getter in the history of the sport and has been addressed as the "God of Cricket" inspiring generations of aspiring cricketers to take up the sport. His presence has led to significant economic gains by the cricketing board and the country as a whole making cricket a Globally accepted Sport.

Mother Teresa[3] chose to dedicate her life in the care of sick and hungry and believed love as the greatest gift that one can give to others specially the poor. In Her Nobel peace prize acceptance speech in the year 1979 in Norway, she said the following words which can touch any soul:

"Lord, grant that I may seek rather to comfort than to be comforted, to understand than to be understood; to love than to be loved; for it is by forgetting self that one finds; it is forgiving that one is forgiven; it is by dying that one awakens to eternal life"

She had a very clear purpose to life which was to dedicate herself in the service of others.

We can take a leaf out of the lives of great leaders like Mother Teresa, Sachin Tendulkar, Vinod Bansal amongst others to commit to a cause in the service of others.

Author Jim Collins[4] in his book Good to Great- published in the year 2001 emphasized on a concept called "first who then what" which he explains as: most companies start with direction first, followed by a vision and strategy and lastly get the people to steer the ship" which isn't the best way. In fact, he suggests first having the right people on the bus, wrong people off the bus and then deciding the direction and course on which the ship needs to be steered. This throws light on the fact that your core identity or who you are is more important than anything else, even more important than the skills, qualifications etc.

Simon Sinek[5] in his book, Start with Why published in the year 2007, talks about the Golden circle where the inner most circle is why, followed by how and then what. He mentions that most people start with what or the goal they want to achieve, then work on the process or how and finally see if their core ideology or why is aligned with the objective they seek, which is wrong.

They must ideally start with why, the purpose, reason, the individuality, who they are deep down as a person or as an organization, what do they stand for, figure that out first.

James Clear[6] also in his book atomic habits published in the year 2018, speaks about outcome-based habits and identity-based habits. Where he explains that people first focus on the outcomes, followed by the process and finally work on their identity which is outside in approach, however they must focus on the inside out approach, starting with the identity first.

If you notice clearly all three authors Jim Collins, Simon Sinek, James clear they are all focusing on one common thing, who you are? Why do you do the things that you do? What do you stand for, what is your individuality, what is your purpose?

These three books combined has sold more than 26 million or 2.6 crores copies worldwide, empowering crores of people across demographics and psychographics on a simple premise of "WHY"- your purpose, your values, what do you believe in, your individuality.

This Universal concept can be seen adopted by every successful organization or people who have made a difference with their work. They started working on their values system first, based on those values came the mission which paved the way for vision.

Today every organization has a very clearly defined Value, Misson and Vision statement and that is the glue which holds people together across geographies within the country and outside.

But let me ask you, what are your values, mission and vision statement? What is it that provides you with direction and motivation to keep going. If you haven't crafted one, now is the time and I will help you do that.

Your values are your deeply held principles which guide your actions and behaviour. Your values determine your identity, who you are and why do you do the things that you do.

If you have done your goal setting exercise, you know what you want to achieve and maybe have a rough idea of how you want to achieve those goals. But here is a quick insight into what happens after the goal setting process.

Research shows that 92% of people fail to achieve their goals.
That means out of a 100 people Only 8 people achieve their defined goals. Remaining 92 do not achieve due to various reasons but the main reason is that their aspirations are not aligned with who they are internally.

Over the years, experimenting with different techniques, I have come to realize that it all boils down to just one word PASSION. And I recently discovered that it is well substantiated by the Hedgehog concept given by Jim Collins. Hedgehog Concep[7]t is followed by many top leaders of the world today.

Jim collings defines the hedgehog concept based on the intersection of 3 circles:

Circle 1 – what is it that you are deeply passionate about

Circle 2- what you can (and cannot) be the best in the world at

Circle 3- what drives your economic engine

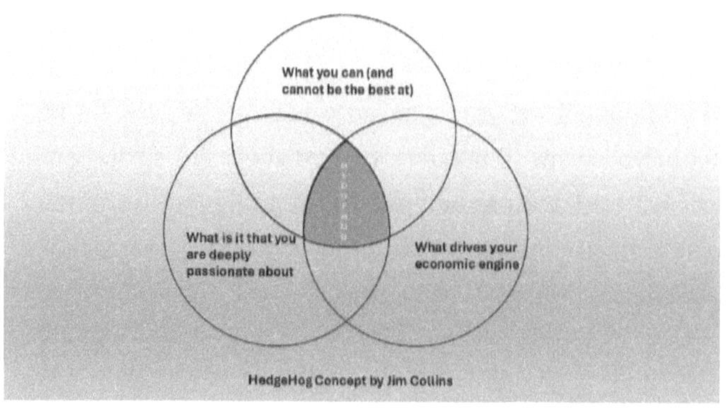

HedgeHog Concept by Jim Collins

Let me give an example: If I woke you up while you are deep asleep and asked to go for a particular actor's movie, you will immediately jump off your bed maybe because you could be a budding actor, director, or a cinematographer. If you woke me up and said, hey Ajay there is a big discount at the bookstore, I would immediately jump off the bed to grab the deal since I am passionate reader. Your business model as an entrepreneur or as an employee having a 9-5 job also must be such, filled with Passion. You must enjoy yourself while you work. if you are cursing yourself as soon as you get up first thing in the morning; oh! I must complete that boring project, I must chase people to get my work done, I hate my work, Only God can save me. Trust me, you will continue to struggle for the rest of your working life because you operate from a paradigm of dissatisfaction and complaints.

1) Circle 1 talks about: Being Deeply passionate about what you do

Here is a quick trick that I follow. I work for myself even while I work for others. In fact, I had the privilege to work with a CEOs of a top Multinational company who used to openly say this in Townhalls: You all must USE the company to fulfil your dreams and aspirations and help the organisation grow as you grow. This is one statement which inspired me to give my best every day and when I did that, I realised my vision overlapped with the vision of the founder. My job satisfaction kept going up with the change in my belief system. My efforts were beneficial to both, the organization that I worked for and for myself as well.

2) Circle 2: What you can (and cannot) be the best in the world at.

You might take a lot of pride in your multitasking abilities. The research says the human brain never multitasks and it reduces the cognitive efficiency over a period leading to lower productivity with impaired focus. This is one of the reasons why people and companies do not grow at a pace that they should ideally grow. You cannot apportion your intensity equally across multiple tasks, you must increase the intensity at one task on which you can be the best in the world at and reduce the intensity on other tasks. You do not want to be called as "Jack of all trades and master of none"

The biggest reason for debacle of most companies and individuals is this one reason, "diversified focus across multiple tasks which never really converges".

Just because you can do something, you don't have to. Specific tasks can be outsourced to specialist who are good at it, you are free to provide direction but mustn't focus on doing the hit and trial yourself.

3) Circle no 3- is what drives your economic engine:

whatever you do you must ensure that it gives you monetary gains. Here you must track the right financial metric. There are various metrics such as base salary, bonus and incentives, total compensation, savings rate, investment growth, net worth, Income to expense ratio, Income to debt ratio and so and so forth. Sometimes the compensation may keep going up but the base in hand salary remains the same. What is that metric which makes sense for you, be mindful of that and increase your focus on that.

Hedgehog Concept is formed by the intersection of these 3 circles and the name Hedgehog is derived from the animal Hedgehog which is known to have a very simple defence mechanism with its thorn like hair spikes that safeguards it from any outside threat. Your idea or approach also must be that simple, something that you can sustain for a long time, something that you are deeply passionate about, something where you can become the best in the world at and finally that something which drives your economic engine.

Crafting our VMVs may not be a one-day process, it is going to take time. It is going to take a lot of self-reflection. How did you react when you met with a failure, when you are pushed into a corner, did you choose the easy way out or did what was right. How do you conduct yourself within the community. How do you treat people who have got nothing to give back to you in return. How do you exercise authority when wielding power in your hand and so on and so forth.

When you ask these questions to yourself, you will uncover your personality, as an individual, and as an organization. You will understand why you do the things that you do and what you can do to improve the how behind the things that you do. Thus, use that as a tool to draft your own values, mission and vision statements. You would soon realize that your efficiency has gone up multifold in no time because now you align your actions and behaviours to the broader outline that you have defined.

We are still living in an age where people are bucketed under the Expenses, and the machines are bucketed under assets. All Human Resource managers openly voice their opinion that employees are the biggest asset of the organization yet none of them will ever go the CFO requesting to make that change. Just because it has been happening for ages doesn't mean it is right. People are the greatest asset of any organization, but not all people are the right people, right people are people with their own values, who align themselves with the organizational values and grow the organization as they grow.

Here are 3 simple ways to find your purpose:

1) Stay Curious:

Most often People have this misconception that the industry they are part of is the best industry to be. The skills they have are the best skills to have. The lifestyle they have is a special one. If you closed your eyes to your surroundings, if you are not mindful of the changes that are happening around you, how do you expect that whatever you are going to do will be adopted by other people. Or whatever you do will make a difference in the lives of people. Sometimes just by being curious and observant we learn more than doing anything in action. Next step is the iteration- how many times do you repeat the process. Sometimes initial couple of months or years may feel boring to you and suddenly you have this eureka moment, a sudden realisation of how you have been doing or looking at the entire scheme of things. Just by being curious you are letting new information form a part of your conscious memory, thus creating an opportunity for your subconscious to take some of this information coupling it with the existing information and showing you a new perspective altogether.

2) Aim to become the best at what you do: The process of becoming best expands your horizon to look at the overall picture. Be it any field sales, marketing, analytics, research, counselling, architecture, social service, coaching or anything else. Find out who are the best people in the world at the field you are looking to excel. Make an approximate calculation-how many times or by what percent they are better than you. for

e.g. If you wanted to become an entrepreneur in electronics industry for a wearable device, find out who is leading the space in that specific field. If it is a publicly traded company, you can get most of the financial as well as non-financial metrics like what is the CTC of the leadership team, what are the CSR initiatives, what is the roadmap, what are the identified risks, what are the policies so on and so forth. Now from doubting to become the best you have got the data points against which you can compare yourself and know what it will take to become the best. You may choose to start from one thing first. Pitting yourself against all things that the best companies do isn't advisable, start with one area first. You can look at one parameter on which you can beat the competition. Early small win will give you the confidence to carry forward. As you embark with this competitive approach you will discover whether your heart is really into it or not, serving as a reminder to do something that you really love and not do something for the sake of doing.

3) Build a state of Internal & External Harmony:

Strive to achieve a balance of internal as well as external harmony. Congruence of the body, mind, heart and spirit first, followed by Congruence with the external people, communities and societies at large. Your body must be such that it can keep up with the constant demands of the work that you do. Mind must be filled with positive & constructive thoughts. Heart must be free of hate and spirit is your clear conscience. Norman Vincent Peale[8] in his book "The power of positive thinking" says the following words to find the way to happiness.

> *"Keep your heart free from hate, your mind from worry. Live simply, expect little, give much. Fill your life with love. Scatter sunshine. Forget self, think others. Do as you wish to be done by"*

Finding a state of internal happiness is essential. If you yourself are feeling stressed and burned out, how can you lead others towards the common good. For this a state of physical, mental, emotional and spiritual harmony is essential. Hector Garcia and Francesco Miralles[9] in their book "Ikigai" the Japanese secret to a long and happy life talks about "The 80% Secret" according to which Japanese say the word "Hara Hachi bu" before or after eating which means something like -fill your belly to only 80%. It is believed that overeating causes the stomach to work overtime, which wears down the body. Thus, to live long with a healthy body, eat less. Mental health is a result of what you read and see. If you condition your mind with good books, right media you will eventually have a sharper mind. Emotional health is more about practicing empathy and inclusiveness with people around you, consider serving others first than your own self, listening not just with ears but also eyes as well. Look at a situation by putting yourself in other's shoes, try to feel what they feel. This way you are more considerate of the feelings and emotions of others as well as yourself.

Chapter Summary:

1) Your purpose is your identity, the reason why you exist. It is the fuel that fires your engine. Who you are? Why do you do the things that you do? What do you stand for, what is your individuality, what is your purpose? Uncover the answer to these questions by continuous self-reflection.

2) Purpose has got nothing to do with age, you can have the realisation in any of the life stages, however it's possible to practice few techniques to find your purpose faster.

3) Most goals fail because people's aspirations are not aligned with who they are internally

4) The Biggest reason for debacle of most companies and individuals is "diversified focus which never really converges"

5) Find your Hedgehog concept, an idea popularised by Jim Collins. It is based on the intersection of 3 circles. Circle one- what is it that you are deeply passionate about, circle two- What you can (and cannot) be the best in the world at, circle three- what drives your economic engine.

6) Stay curious- Curiosity open the door to new streams of knowledge and broadens the horizons of thought. It also brings a new perspective to look at things.

7) Aim to be the best at what you do- while you purse to become the best in your domain, the realisation to continue or change stream becomes crystal clear based on the gap you see between yourself and somebody else who is on top of the ladder

8) Build a state of internal and external Harmony- strive to achieve a state of internal congruence where all four dimensions body, mind, heart and spirit are aligned with your purpose externally.

9) Write your own Values, Misson and Vision statements

4. Framework Based Approach

"Out of clutter, find simplicity. From discord, find harmony. In the middle of difficulty lies opportunity."

Albert Einstein

Chapter 1 *talks* about being Resilient, Chapter 2 shows the methods to reframe every setback positively, chapter 3 elaborates on finding purpose and doing what we love deeply. In this chapter we will understand how to increase our effectiveness in whatever we do by following a structured methodology.

When I moved into Sales Operations from Sales role a couple of years back, I had to build a lot of new skills from scratch, especially business analytics, Customer relationship management, strategic planning, process optimization, & Collaboration. Communication was never a concern, having done my schooling from one of the best schools in the country, that is Doon International School, Dehradun.

I had worked independently so far but now I had to work alongside the CEO and Chairman, implement strategies on ground. Collaborate with functional heads, get their input, align their interests, align interest of the sales and marketing team, summarize all that had transpired for management review and keep the grind going.

 I will always be indebted to the CEO for pushing me out of my comfort zone. He abundantly credited me for the tasks that I was doing, acknowledging my efforts multiple times in team meetings both at peer and management level. He extended his trust that I will come good with the projects assigned. His Leadership style was unique, not something I had experienced before with any of my previous Bosses. He had seen potential in me, which I hadn't realized about myself yet.

I felt pressurized, yet in a positive way. But the ground reality was, I wasn't good at the skills needed to consistently deliver on projects. What do I do?

Remember from chapter 1 right, Resilience is the greatest predictor of success than any other skill. I have always felt that very strongly. I have always believed *I CAN DO IT.*

So can you, It's all in the mindset. It's self-belief that has led to the greatest of personal achievements, not academic credentials. Otherwise only the sons and daughters of the privileged few will make the cut.

At this point in time, I did not have any system or method to Fastrack my learning process. It was just plain hard work. I started first by mastering Zoho CRM, a customer relationship management software, to manage databases, communicate with leads, Reporting & analytics, Rule based controls and a host of other features. Very soon I implemented the software for 50 plus people in the company, training them on how to apply it in their day-to-day workings.

This was the first major win to boost my confidence. Parallelly, I continued to improve my Microsoft excel skills and went on to clear the exam for "Microsoft certified Excel expert". This fuelled the fire raging inside me. I became unstoppable after that! I Remember telling my dad once to google my name with Microsoft certified excel expert and it was the first result that popped up with my image on his mobile. His expression filled with pride said it all, as usual he did not used many words and finished his appreciation with 2 words, "Good son".

Mastering other skills like Strategic planning, Collaboration, Process Optimization wasn't very difficult after that. I just followed the grind, studied most of the days after work, during the weekends, whenever I could find time, I committed to learning something new most of my time. After 6 months into the role the Vice

President of the company said, Ajay since you are taking 35-40% of my workload it gives me some leverage, I can now increase my focus on other strategic requirements for the company. After about 2 years in the role, I got promoted to Director of Sales Operations having developed sharp acumen across all my responsibilities.

I wasn't feeling pressure at work now. The work wasn't demanding anymore. The tasks that used to take me 3-4 hours to complete, I was able to do them in under 30 mins. At this point of time the grind had become a part of me, I wanted to keep learning new things and my hunger has been on the rise ever since. I learnt new skills outside of professional commitments, continuing the habit even today and this process had led me to identify my purpose to spread my voice to those who are struggling in their lives either professionally or personally, so they can become the best version of themselves wherever they are in whichever capacity they work. This book is one humble attempt sharing the principles I have discovered.

Over the years I have come to build frameworks that have saved me a lot of time and energy and I will talk about how you can build the same for yourself. Before that let's understand what Frameworks are.

Frameworks are the tools that simplify the way you go about doing any task. They help you align your action consistently for innumerable times, preventing the chances of failure or delay in the outcomes you seek.

No organization or individual can accurately execute a task without following a defined framework. It can be in multiple forms like a chart, flowsheets, process manual, visual markers or even mental notes. It can be in any form possible however the main objective is to help execute a task in a faster, error-free, & scalable manner.

Imagine if you have to go to your study room from the bedroom or from the study room to the parking lot without touching anything. Can you cover the distance without colliding with anything in between. Well, the chances are very slim no matter how many times you have walked the path. What if you are asked to go by sensing the objects in between. In that case you may possibly make the distance but not accurately unless you practice a few times. However, what if you made a framework of walking 6 steps in one direction, felt the object, took another couple of steps in another direction, sensed the object and voila you have reached the destination, with eyes closed. This is nothing but system based or framework-based thinking. Planning your actions in accordance with a set sequence of steps, time and again for uniformity & consistency in results. If you requested your friend to get a pair of T-shirts from your house even if he hadn't visited your house before, he could execute the task with great ease, provided you have given him a framework to follow.

As Humans we are the smartest species on this planet, over the years as we have evolved a lot, so have the ways in which we conduct ourselves. Our ancestors had very basic necessities like food, shelter, and clothing, however, generations later our requirements and the means in which we achieve them have drastically changed. Civilization started with the hunting age, then moved to farming, and finally to industrialization. Today food is no longer scarce, it is abundantly available to most if not all. However, the method in which we get the food on the plate has changed. Similarly for the working class of people, and the knowledge workers, the way we search for information, consume, and comprehend has evolved considerably.

Today information is democratized. That means everyone has access to quality information, both rich and poor. Yet the Gap is at Execution. How do you make sense of the information you have is equally important. Thus, the use of systems or frameworks becomes important. How is it that 2 people studying in the same institute, under the same teacher, achieve different outcomes right after college. one gets a package of crores; other hardly makes a few lakhs even though they both specialize in the same field. The difference is in their thought process, One thinks based on frameworks, other thinks based on General knowledge.

You may have read about a hundred techniques, however if you cannot recall them in a time of need, you haven't really mastered those techniques. The way you remember things and apply them in action is based on the framework that you have applied in the personal capacity and based on the framework applied there will be difference in outcomes. The outcomes may also vary in terms of their quality and time taken to deliver them.

Let me ask you a simple question: what do you do first thing in the morning when you get up?

Everyone has got their own routine in the morning. There are a host of things like Gym workout, running outdoors, Yoga, Mindfulness, Newspaper reading, outdoor walk, watching news, playing a sport etc. Based on demographics and psychographics the interest varies. However, there is one thing very common across the generations starting from silent generation to Generation Alpha, that is *NOT PLANNING ACTIVITIES FOR THE DAY* outside of the regular things that will anyways be done.

There are 6 generations of people:

    i.   Silent generation (1928-1945)
   ii.   Baby Boomers (1946-1964)
  iii.   Generation X (1965-1980)
  iv.   Millennials or Gen Y (1981-1996)
   v.   Generation Z (1997-2012)
  vi.   Generation Alpha (2013-2025)

Today close to 3-5 different generations of people are staying together in one house. Yet there is one surprising thing common amongst each of the generation that is a lack of PLAN on how they are going to make the best use of the day. You may say that you like to be present in the moment and take on things as they come, which is good, but you can do better. As per a report, it is said that more than 75% of people proceed through their day without having a Daily plan. That means less than 25% of people are involved in the daily planning process.

Without Frameworks no industry can Operate today, let us take an example of a few industries:

a. In Technological space some of the commonly used frameworks are: Agile, Scrum, DevOps etc
b. In Business and strategy commonly, used frameworks are SWOT (strength-weakness-opportunity-threat), SMART (specific-measurable-achievable-realistic-timebound), STAR (situation-task-action-result), OKRs (Objective and key results)
c. In Marketing commonly used frameworks are 4Ps(product-price-place-promotion), 7Ps (product-price-place-promotion-people-process-physical evidence, AIDA (awareness-interest-desire-action), STP (segmentation-targeting-positioning) etc
d. In Human resources commonly used frameworks are 5Ps(philosophy-policies-programs-practices-performance), OTP (onboarding to productivity time), Attrition rate, Average life cycle of an employee etc

The question that arises is when small & large companies across industries have adapted their entire working on frameworks, why can't we as individuals develop a personalised framework for ourselves. It is not important that you follow a framework that already exists in the market. You can make a framework based on your own lifestyle, habits, and preferences.

The Ground Reality is: No two People think alike, yet most of them end up very much alike, with a life of mediocrity. Thus, give a structure, format, framework to everything that you do, personalised to you and achieve the greatness that you seek.

Every action has 3 parts, beginning, middle and the end. As you begin, never let go of the sight where you want to be, i.e. the end goal. Being mindful of the end goal prevents distraction and even if newer methods present themselves, thoughts re-align, picking and choosing only that which furthers the quest, ignoring the rest as noise.

Here are example scenarios to get you thinking. The idea is to break down the ask into smaller manageable pieces and create a new system based on personal preferences, skills etc.

Scenario 1: Let us say you are the owner of a 1000-member company. You are supposed to deliver a 20-minute talk to boost the morale of your employees and must deliver the speech without any digital aid. How would you go about it?

It can be broken down into 2 parts

    i.   Write the speech
        a.   Follow a sub-framework while jotting your thoughts
            i.   Opening statement

        ii.   Introduction
        iii. Body/Message
        iv. Conclusion
  ii.   Deliver the speech
      a.   Follow a sub-framework while delivering your talk
        i.   Pitch
        ii.   Pace
        iii. Pause
        iv. Body Language
  iii.   Introspect what has gone well, what could be improved

The framework applied here is Opening + IMC + PPP + Body language. There is a beginning, middle and end (end is just introspection).

You can categorize this objective into 3 parts. Then Under the Broader framework divided these into subparts so remembrance and recollection both becomes easier. It is extremely difficult to remember your talk if you haven't structured your thoughts while writing the script and are not being mindful of the body language you want to demonstrate. Your natural personality in terms of the way you talk, the way you stand, and the way you react to a question will take precedence if you don't consciously try to change it. Your personality speaks more about you than the words you speak. To change the way in which you are being perceived by others you must change the way you look at yourself. Self-Reflection is the tool that you need to understand in depth about your own personality. Again, how do you self-reflect is also important, Frameworks are needed for that too, to have a sequence in the way you let your thoughts unfold inside your mind. It is famously said, "a man is what is thinks of all day". While you self-reflect to understand your personality and get carried away thinking about your favourite holiday destination, your focus has shifted. So, stay focused by leveraging a self-made framework.

Scenario 2: You have started learning a new spoken language yet have not been able to make much progress due to the complexity involved. How can you fast track your learning process?

Here is a simple framework that you can use to impress upon your memory in as many ways as possible.

i.   Read aloud and Practice to impress upon your auditory and visual senses together
ii.   Record your words and listen back to them to impress upon auditory senses
iii. Make notes to impress upon your visual memory
iv.   Join a community to interact with peers- this also increases positive peer pressure
v.   Practice as many times as possible, nothing beats practice

Here the mental framework used is to impress upon as many senses as possible with repeated practice. There could be many more ways to master the language, yet all of them will finally lead to repetition,

repetition by practicing more, repetition by impressing upon as many senses as possible, repeating as frequently as possible. If you keep doing something for long enough, your muscles tend to remember those movements and it becomes part of your muscular memory as well.

Scenario 3: You have Negotiation meeting coming up, with a large client. Everything is done Except the Pricing Discussion. How do you prepare the next steps.

Here is a simple framework that you can use:
i. Mentally note the bottom-line number below which you wouldn't go
ii. Understand that you have the power to walk away at any moment of time
iii. The agreement must be mutually beneficial. If it only favours you and the other party realises that the deal will not proceed forward. Strive to balance the interest of both parties.
iv. You can choose to agree or disagree with other party's however never ignore anything that they say during the negotiations, be vigilant.
v. Watch their body language. Are the words matching with the body language that they are demonstrating.
vi. Be Respectful no matter what.

Here the mental framework used is not to go below the bottom line with a win-win mindset, having a beginning middle and the end clearly defined.

The above example scenarios encompass a broader categorization of any situation into beginning, middle and end and further drills it down to sub parts. However, each problem may require a different point of view and should be approached differently.

When you list down the steps that need to be done, your effectiveness automatically gets increased. The purpose behind listing the steps is to bring your attention to the importance of having a structure in everything you do. This reduces the cognitive load significantly since you are not pressuring your brain to recall everything you need at every critical point in time.

Here are 3 simple ways to build a personalized framework:

1. Start with Outcome, then break the outcome into small wins:
   a. Often people are tirelessly working in a direction in the false anticipation that something magical will happen very soon. Well, it may or may not! You cannot just wait for things to happen to you, you must define the outcome you want to achieve. Outcomes can be qualitative or quantitative. Qualitative means you may say I want to become rich, quantitative mean you will say I want to earn 1 crore rupees and become rich. There is a difference in both. Make the goal as tangible and

realistic as possible. Whenever you take an initiative, ask yourself, how is that action taking you closer to the goal you have defined. 5 Out of 10 times this one simple question will change your approach towards the initiative you were about to take. When you have the end goal clearly in mind, you will never get derailed. Even though you may get distracted sometimes, your desire will realign your focus, however, to persist with a focused approach for an extended period you need a quantitative outcome broken down into small parts. So, each small win gives you the motivation to keep pushing. You can divide the tasks into smaller more achievable goals. No task is impossible if you can break it down to smaller manageable pieces. The way you chunk the process can be based on your capabilities and resources that you have at your disposal. This simple art of chunking is a framework in itself.

2. Follow the rule of sequencing and association:

If you are used to working on a spreadsheet, then the moment you apply sort ascending or descending on a number or name, it becomes so much easier to find what you had been looking for. With advanced excel tools you can also do conditional formatting which colour codes the data into 3 colours, light dark and darkest, helping you find odd one out within seconds.

Such is The Human Brain- it loves sequences, and Association. In the field of memory building, association is the strongest principle there is. You can ask any memory expert; he wouldn't deny this. You can store large amounts of important information just by associating one piece of information with another. Sequencing is not association. In Sequencing Order matters, whereas in association order does not matter. Sequencing is linear or stepwise whereas association is relational, or pattern based. Applying either of it individually or together will make your task much easier.

3. Practice, Practice, Practice:

You can have the world's best trick at your disposal however if you haven't practiced your craft you are bound to forget them sooner rather than later. Of course, the retention of information will be longer since you have segmented, sequenced and associated in a particular fashion but without practice even this will be forgotten. Practice supersedes everything! As you practice you will notice, your comprehension power keeps going up, you will start forming pattern unconsciously feeding the conscious brain automatically. Human brains are the most sophisticated tool in the world, yet very few have mastered it.

Every Great Leader has followed some or the other framework as per his preference. Today, it is not uncommon for leaders across different domains to share their opinions on the ideal strategy to achieve an outcome. Let me explain, if the host asked a question such as, "what is the quickest way to build wealth today" in a panel of 3 experts, there is a chance that there could be three unique answers or there could be an overlap. However, the suggestion would be followed differently by different people. Response to execution will be based on the existing knowledge base someone has. If the expert answered, "the fastest way to build wealth is though the compounding and diversification" all you need is to diversify your funds across different asset class and let the magic unfold. Pause for a moment and think, what did you understand by that answer and what are you going to do about it. Diversification means different for different people. Someone might invest in real estate, gold and emergency liquid funds. Somone might invest in index funds, exchange trades funds and bonds etc. Everyone has their own paradigm of looking at things and the one who can look beyond the same old tricks will grow his money significantly. It's all in the perspective. One thought idea today can be the difference between you and your friend down the line in 15 years. That one idea can be general advice from an expert that both of implemented at the same time, yet one has 15X More wealth than the other. The message I want to drive here is, everyone has a unique perspective at looking at things and the one who continuously upskills will benefit the maximum even with general advice, because the meaning derived is based on the competency someone has. When you keep building new skills, you continue to upgrade your comprehension power and the ability to draw insights from complex situations becomes much easier. So, whatever you see and hear will all contribute to the outcome you seek.

This new way of looking at things can be based on an upgraded thought process which is nothing but framework-based thinking. Frameworks may initially be cumbersome to build and implement, however once implemented the results they produce are mind-boggling.

The fastest way to grow is to emulate those who are successful. Sometimes you emulate people who are in the same industry and sometime outside your domain. The intention is to achieve success by implementing their advice as is or with slight modifications. Yet I said to grow, not keep growing! You cannot keep growing following the same 5 steps another person is following. The flaws eventually tend to show themselves, reducing the effectiveness of your strategy. So, the best thing to do is to be agile, keep an open mind, and build your own framework after studying the gaps in the market. I am not suggesting that there cannot be any similarities with the existing frameworks. There will always be some overlaps, yet the differentiation comes in the way of execution. The way you look at product design could be far different from your best friend working in a similar industry for another company, it's all about perspective, the past conditioning that both of you may have.

Few more suggestions based on my Experience:

❖ Start on an idea, but don't rush through the process of completing it. A lot of time people might recommend time-bound activities, and it is good, however as per my practice I only do that when I am really crunch on time. The idea incubates in the mind after starting on it. For e.g. If I have to give a motivational talk, I start writing the script but don't aim to finish it in one sitting. In fact, I let the idea brew in mind's palace for some time, this improves the quality of thoughts. Thus, I start writing the script at-least 6-7 days in advance for maximum effectiveness.

❖ Most often when you start with something, a new business, a new relationship, a new responsibility, do not assume you know everything needed to thrive into that role. Most ideas when started weren't compete and were full of flaws. The idea is improvised upon slowly taking in feedback from as many people as possible, this process can take years on some occasions. If you have an idea, let it brew in the mind's palace for as long as possible, ponder over it whenever you can, take feedback from trusted sources, integrate that feedback, improvise and then make the launch. Similarly at relationships, you wouldn't really know something in just a few takes, patterns begin to emerge gradually about the people you deal with. Don't be quick to judge someone, even if you knew body language reading skills.

❖ Dr Pavan Joshi is his book Design your thinking gives 5 step frameworks to problem solving which I have found to be very effective.

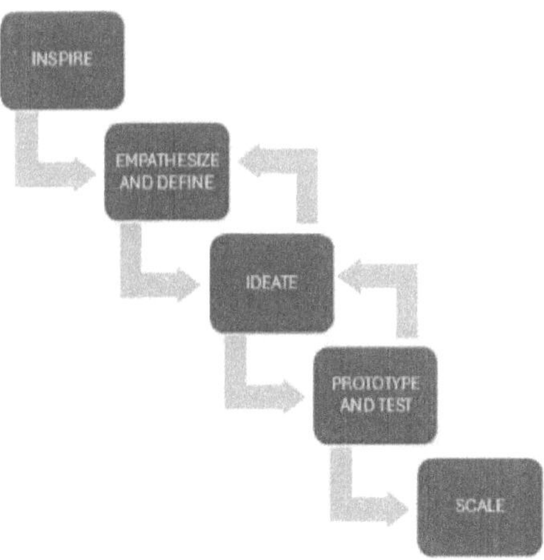

Inspire stage helps determine the why behind the problem solving, why does it need to be addressed. Empathize and Define stage is bringing a human centric approach to problem solving by defining the boundaries of the problem. Ideate stage helps generate large no of ideas (involves focusing on quantity over quality which is a little counterintuitive however it is important to have as many options as possible). The Prototype and Test stage are about picking the most promising ideas and testing them. Scale Stage is finally when the idea is implemented, and its impact is realized.

Chapter summary:

1. Frameworks are the tools that simplify the way you go about doing any tasks. They can be in any form possible however their main objective is to help execute a task in a faster, error free, & scalable manner
2. framework-based thinking lets you plan your actions in accordance with a set sequence of steps, repeatedly for uniformity & consistency in results.
3. There is patten around us and will continue to be, no matter how evolved we become.
4. Difference between a successful and not successful individual is that one follows a framework-based thinking whereas other follows a generalised method of thinking.
5. There are well established frameworks in each industry, it is high time we developed a

personalised framework based upon our own need, preference and skills.

6. Start with an outcome and then break the process down to smaller more achievable pieces. Make the processes as quantifiable as possible.

7. Question yourself as you initiate something new- How is it contributing towards the outcome you have in mind. If supports positively, then proceed, else Re-align your focus.

8. Follow the rule of sequencing and association. These can be applied in any kind of situation. Sequencing is linear or stepwise, whereas association is relational or patten based.

9. Practice often to hard code the framework into your subconscious.

10. Everyone has a different paradigm of looking at things, one who can think differently can make a difference.

11. The fastest way to grow is emulation, but not to keep growing. For that you need to be agile and nimble footed with your own frameworks based on the gaps identified.

5. Follow the Rule of 90 Days

"Lack of direction, not lack of time, is the problem. We all have 24-hour-days."

Zig Ziglar

So far, you have learnt to be resilient and positive, driven by your purpose, following a structured methodology. In this chapter we will learn about consistency, how long should we sustain something to make a behavioural habit change.

Some time in May 2021 I observed that I couldn't keep track of my activities. I kept forgetting where I left off last time, while juggling between multiple tasks. This led to reduced effectiveness & efficiency and got me worried. After a month, On 1st June 2021 I started recording all my activities on a excel sheet. Though I don't recall the exact reason that prompted me to do this, being overwhelmed with multiple tasks was definitely one reason. Second could have been my curiosity towards Microsoft excel at that time, I kept finding opportunities to implement and master new tricks. Thus, I ended up making a personal dashboard for key activities.

It's 939 days(>2.5Years) today as I'm writing this chapter, and I have continued with this habit of updating the daily activity tracker. The initial 3 months were very difficult to maintain this monotonous habit, yet I persisted, today it only takes 5 minutes to update. Even today, I feel a rush of Dopamine every time I look at my chart. I have attached Table 1 below for your reference.

I analyzed 3 metrics- first what has been the trend for last 3 weeks, then last 6 weeks and finally cumulatively since the time I had started. Just one glance at this chart and I was set for the next week. I had defined minimum hours per activity and the percentage achievement week by week. This gave me a clear indication about where I was struggling or exceeding the benchmarks.

Table 1:

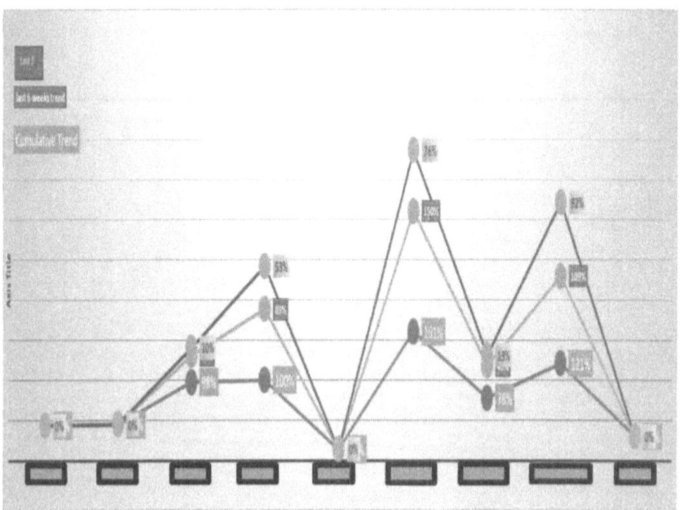

Over a period, I have kept improvising on the initial model, but the core idea remained the same throughout i.e. to understand my effectiveness across multiple tasks by measuring the amount of time spent.

There were further upsides to this that I did not anticipate early on. As I progressed, I uncovered a lot of insights that wouldn't have been possible otherwise. I could clearly see my effectiveness increasing across multiple areas.

Thereafter, I made a 168-hour weekly tracker to get a sense of the entire 24 hours. This was just an extension of the previous model.

Table 2:

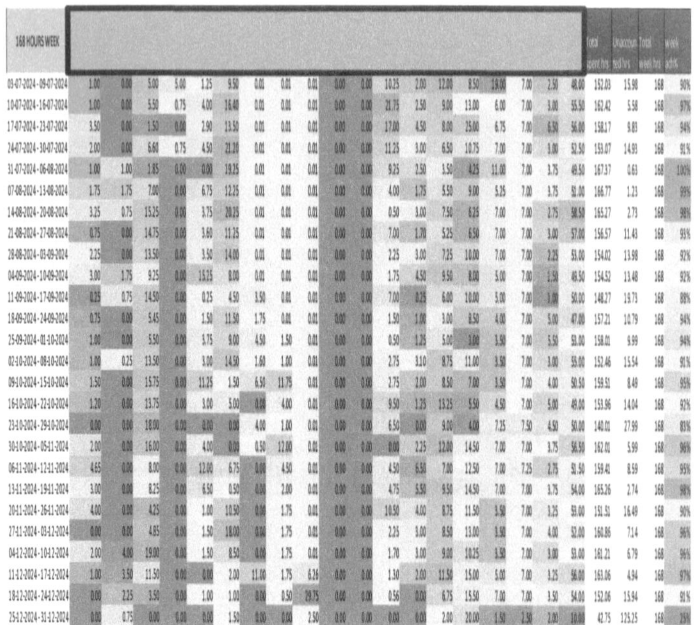

168 HOURS WEEK																				Total spent hrs	Unaccounted hrs	Total week hrs	week activ%
03-07-2024 - 09-07-2024	1.00	0.00	5.00	5.00	1.25	9.50	0.01	0.01	0.01	0.00	0.00	10.25	2.00	12.00	8.50	19.00	7.00	2.50	48.00	152.03	15.98	168	90%
10-07-2024 - 16-07-2024	1.00	0.00	5.50	0.75	4.00	16.40	0.01	0.01	0.01	0.00	0.00	21.75	2.50	9.00	13.00	6.00	7.00	3.00	55.50	162.42	5.58	168	97%
17-07-2024 - 23-07-2024	3.50	0.00	1.50	0.00	2.90	13.50	0.01	0.01	0.01	0.00	0.00	17.00	4.50	8.00	25.00	6.75	7.00	6.50	56.00	158.17	9.83	168	94%
24-07-2024 - 30-07-2024	2.00	0.00	6.60	0.75	4.50	21.20	0.01	0.01	0.01	0.00	0.00	11.25	3.00	6.50	10.75	7.00	7.00	3.00	52.50	153.07	14.93	168	91%
31-07-2024 - 06-08-2024	1.00	1.00	1.85	0.00	0.00	19.25	0.01	0.01	0.01	0.00	0.00	9.25	2.50	3.50	4.25	11.00	7.00	3.75	49.50	167.37	0.63	168	100%
07-08-2024 - 13-08-2024	1.75	1.75	7.00	0.00	6.75	12.25	0.01	0.01	0.01	0.00	0.00	4.00	1.75	5.50	9.00	5.25	7.00	3.75	51.00	166.77	1.23	168	99%
14-08-2024 - 20-08-2024	3.25	0.75	15.25	0.00	3.75	20.25	0.01	0.01	0.01	0.00	0.00	0.50	3.00	7.50	6.25	7.00	7.00	2.75	58.50	165.27	2.73	168	98%
21-08-2024 - 27-08-2024	0.75	0.00	14.75	0.00	3.60	11.25	0.01	0.01	0.01	0.00	0.00	7.00	1.70	5.25	6.50	7.00	7.00	3.00	57.00	156.57	11.43	168	93%
28-08-2024 - 03-09-2024	2.25	0.00	13.50	0.00	3.50	14.00	0.01	0.01	0.01	0.00	0.00	2.25	3.00	7.25	10.00	7.00	7.00	2.25	53.00	154.02	13.98	168	92%
04-09-2024 - 10-09-2024	3.00	1.75	9.25	0.00	15.25	8.00	0.01	0.01	0.01	0.00	0.00	1.75	4.50	9.50	8.00	5.00	7.00	1.50	49.50	154.52	13.48	168	92%
11-09-2024 - 17-09-2024	0.25	0.75	14.50	0.00	0.25	4.50	3.50	0.01	0.01	0.00	0.00	7.00	0.25	6.00	10.00	5.00	7.00	3.00	50.00	148.27	19.73	168	88%
18-09-2024 - 24-09-2024	0.75	0.00	5.45	0.00	1.50	11.50	1.75	0.01	0.01	0.00	0.00	1.50	1.00	3.00	8.50	4.00	7.00	5.00	47.00	157.21	10.79	168	94%
25-09-2024 - 01-10-2024	1.00	0.00	5.50	0.00	3.75	9.00	4.50	1.50	0.01	0.00	0.00	0.50	1.25	5.00	3.00	3.50	7.00	5.50	53.00	158.01	9.99	168	94%
02-10-2024 - 08-10-2024	1.00	0.25	13.50	0.00	3.00	14.50	1.60	1.00	0.01	0.00	0.00	2.75	3.10	8.75	11.00	3.50	7.00	3.00	55.00	152.46	15.54	168	91%
09-10-2024 - 15-10-2024	1.50	0.00	15.75	0.00	11.25	1.50	6.50	11.75	0.01	0.00	0.00	2.75	2.00	8.50	7.00	3.50	7.00	4.00	50.50	159.51	8.49	168	95%
16-10-2024 - 22-10-2024	1.20	0.00	13.75	0.00	3.00	5.00	0.00	4.00	0.01	0.00	0.00	9.50	1.25	13.25	5.50	4.50	7.00	5.00	49.00	153.96	14.04	168	92%
23-10-2024 - 29-10-2024	0.00	0.00	18.00	0.00	0.00	0.00	4.00	1.00	0.01	0.00	0.00	6.50	0.00	9.00	4.00	7.25	7.50	4.50	50.00	140.01	27.99	168	83%
30-10-2024 - 05-11-2024	2.00	0.00	16.00	0.00	4.00	0.00	0.50	12.00	0.01	0.00	0.00	0.00	2.25	12.00	14.50	7.00	7.00	3.75	56.50	162.01	5.99	168	96%
06-11-2024 - 12-11-2024	4.65	0.00	8.00	0.00	12.00	6.75	0.00	4.50	0.01	0.00	0.00	4.50	6.50	7.00	12.50	7.00	7.25	2.75	51.50	159.41	8.59	168	95%
13-11-2024 - 19-11-2024	3.00	0.00	8.25	0.00	6.50	0.50	0.00	2.00	0.01	0.00	0.00	4.75	5.50	9.50	14.50	7.00	7.00	3.75	54.00	165.26	2.74	168	98%
20-11-2024 - 26-11-2024	4.00	0.00	4.25	0.00	1.00	10.50	0.00	1.75	0.01	0.00	0.00	10.50	4.00	8.75	11.50	3.50	7.00	3.25	53.00	151.51	16.49	168	90%
27-11-2024 - 03-12-2024	0.00	0.00	4.85	0.00	1.50	18.00	0.00	1.75	0.01	0.00	0.00	2.25	3.00	8.50	13.00	3.50	7.00	4.00	52.00	160.86	7.14	168	96%
04-12-2024 - 10-12-2024	2.00	4.00	19.00	0.00	1.50	8.50	0.00	1.75	0.01	0.00	0.00	1.70	3.00	9.00	10.25	3.50	7.00	3.00	53.00	161.21	6.79	168	96%
11-12-2024 - 17-12-2024	1.00	3.50	11.50	0.00	0.00	2.00	11.00	1.75	6.26	0.00	0.00	1.30	2.00	11.50	15.00	5.00	7.00	3.25	56.00	163.06	4.94	168	97%
18-12-2024 - 24-12-2024	0.00	2.25	3.50	0.00	1.00	1.00	0.00	0.50	29.75	0.00	0.00	0.56	0.00	6.75	15.50	7.00	7.00	3.50	54.00	152.06	15.94	168	91%
25-12-2024 - 31-12-2024	0.00	0.75	0.00	0.00	0.00	1.50	0.00	0.00	2.50	0.00	0.00	0.00	0.00	2.00	20.00	1.50	2.50	2.00	10.00	42.75	125.25	168	25%

(few columns have been hidden to reduce the size of the chart; header containing the activity names has been greyed out)

Table 2 is an actual snapshot of my weekly tracker, where I know exactly how much time I have given to each task. On top of that I have just applied conditional formatting which makes it easier to find insights. There are some activities which are in complete dark-they signify that I haven't spent any time on them in the last 6 months. You can see two columns since July to dec 2024 which are completely red (having 0.00 readings). There are some activities where I have maintained a streak of more than 90 days, which is the 6th column from the left. Also, there are a few columns where I have maintained consistency for 40-45 days then taken a break and started again.

There were weeks where I was able to map out more than 98% of the overall time. But it has only happened 4 weeks out of 25 weeks, excluding the last week of December. For about 25 weeks (approx. 6 months) there are 10.5 hours unaccounted for. I don't know where I invested or wasted those 10.5 hours. By the way I am not keeping a minute-to-minute track, it is just at the end of the day 5-minute activity before going to bed. This gives me a holistic view of everything happening in my life. For e.g.:

Should I increase time with books and other resources for personal development...
Should I reduce time with movies and social media in leisure activities...
Do I need to sleep more...
Have I been missing gym often...
Have I done justice to other smaller commitments...
What has been my professional time commitment and how has It served me...
Have I been procrastinating few items needlessly...
Has my new learning initiatives added to my professional acumen...

And many more insights. The crux of the matter is that Everyone in the world has got the same 168 hours. The richest person of the world and you yourself. What separates you from him is the way you manage your 168 hours. I am not guaranteeing that you can become world's most successful individual by managing your time more judiciously, but I can guarantee that you will start to see your routine in 5X magnification and stop doing that which are pure timewasters. Your productivity will multiply after 3-6 months, people will start to observe the change in you but will never figure out this simple hack behind that change. You will rarely miss any deadline after that and will also be able to take a command of your life. Time is the most valuable resource there is but very few people truly understand it. Time gone by is money left on the table. In fact, it is more valuable than money. Money can be earned back but not the time.

Rule of 90 days simply means to continue with your endeavours for at least 90 days and then deciding the future course of action. Many a times we take on a new project and abandon it midway because we don't find it interesting enough or don't see it leading to an outcome beneficial to us. It means to sustain for at least for 90 days, even if the initial impressions aren't suiting our style or needs. This rule can be applied in most situations in our day-to-day life, like Business, Relationships, Health, Finances etc.

I have come to realise its power after recording each of my activities for more than two and half years. It is a very robust tool if applied in a systematic way. The only thing you need to do is make a proper format to capture your day-to-day activities in whichever tool you are comfortable.

Here is a sample that you can use in Microsoft excel:

Date	Activity1 Target (in hrs)	Activity1 Ach (in hrs)	Activity 1 Ach %	Activity 2 Target (in hrs)	Activity 2 Ach (in hrs)	Activity 2 Ach %
27-12-2024	2	1.5	75%	1.5	1.5	100%
28-12-2024	2	1	50%	1.5	2	133%
29-12-2024	2	1.75	87.5%	1.5	2.25	150%
30-12-2024	2	2.25	112.5%	1.5	1.75	116.5%
31-12-2024	2	1	50%	1.5	1.5	100%
01-01-2025	2	.5	25%	1.5	1	66.5%
02-01-2025	2	.25	12.5%	1.5	1	66.5%
Weekly Report	14	8.25	59%	10.5	11	105%

As per the sample data, the Achievement percent for Activity 1 for the week (Dec 27-Jan 2nd) is 59% whereas for Activity 2 it's 105%. If you are good with spreadsheets, you may do the total calculation though pivot tables (by grouping the dates for 7 days). Pivot table will make your report dynamic, so you don't have to summarize the data week after week.

Here you might be compelled to track everything by minute, do not get into that trap else it would bore you out. I would recommend defining the broad categories under which every activity falls. Second keep the number of categories between 4-7 maximum in the initial days, then as you go, keep adding more activities to the tracker. This is so; you do get burnt in the process of too much data entry. As you increase the fields, remember that as Humans we cannot possibly do twenty activities on a day-to-day basis. There will be trade-offs as we progress based on the urgency and importance of the situation. Just because you have a field for tracking does not mean you have to update that every day, each task must be treated on its own merit. Down the line you may also notice doing a few tasks that were not planned for. These could be your hidden inclinations, that slowly tend to show themselves. As I mentioned earlier, the purpose of the tracker is not just to record everything but also to provide you with insights into your own lifestyle that you would have missed otherwise.

This will show you things about yourself that have been hidden all along. In chapter 1 you learnt the techniques for self-reflection through Journaling, meditation and questioning your actions. A mentor or coach usually understands their students first, before prescribing anything by means of observation, noting down patterns in thoughts and behaviour. Chapter on Resilience, Positive Reframing, finding your purpose empowered you with tools to understand your own internal state first. Chapter on "Framework based Approach" provided you tools to structure your life by thinking differently, thinking of outcome first coupling with techniques of association & sequencing. The last four chapter's insight combined with this chapter with give you a solid Launchpad to achieve anything in life.

There is one more rule that is extensively talked about i.e. "21-day rule".
"Accept my 21 days challenge to transform your life!" is a common marketing pitch for companies and freelancers alike. The actual behavioural change doesn't happen in 21 days, it takes varying amount of time for different individuals for different tasks. Let us understand the origins of the 21-day Rule: Dr Maltz a plastic surgeon generalised that on an average it took his patients 21-days to accept their new look after surgery. Somehow it got popularised by one expert to another without validating its scientific basis. The actual study on behaviour change was done by University College London headed by Dr Phillipa Lally[1] Who found that on an average it took 66 days for a new behaviour to become automatic. However, there can be limitations to this study as well, since it was only done on 96 Individuals. At the same time, she reported that habit formation may take anywhere between 18-254 days depending upon the complexity of the habit and individual's environment and motivations.
Some people are applying the 21-day rule in Health and fitness with their Exercise routine & Eating habits. Some in Productivity improvement by setting up to do list first thing in the morning or organizing their table first thing. Some in finance by reading about stocks and financial news, some in book reading etc. Everybody has their own ways of using this and they are following it with the hope that it will lead to a behaviour change. But scientifically this is not proven to make a behaviour

automatic in 21 days rather it takes different time for different individuals based on multiple factors.

As per Research it is found that only 75% people stick with their new year resolutions till the end of first week and only 8-20% people go on to achieve their resolutions. The second Friday of January is also termed as quitters' day since many a people abandon their goals by this time. The biggest reason for the lapse in commitment is misalignment with who they are internally. To understand your identity, revisit the chapter on "finding your purpose". To recapitulate it suggests, only that can be sustained which is driven by a clear purpose.

You can choose to apply the 90 Days rule in any of your life situations and the outcome will be far more pleasing than you can anticipate. In Health & wellness, finance & investing, Relationships, work life balance, financial stability and independence, Career and professional growth, Personal development, Travel and lifestyle and so on and so forth. The applications are immense.

Application of "Rule of 90 Days"

1. Relationships:
   a. Relationships are driven by Trust and Commitment. Most people commit too soon into a new relationship. Thereafter, realise they have made a mistake. Sometimes you may get attracted to someone based on just one

impression. That one impression can be a face to face connect, a telephone call, or any other medium of engagement. Sometime the engagements may continue for few days or couple of weeks. Reality is, we form a perspective too soon without giving other person a chance to show themselves fully. Some people immediately come out as harsh, transactional, on the face type yet their behaviour may just be situational. Some people are very pleasing on the face and are emphatic yet resort to evil means behind the door. Some people are genuinely caring but are misunderstood because they are introverts. Humans are the most complex organisms, and even though we have evolved with new techniques of reading people like assessing body language, tone, pitch, voice quality etc to gauge authenticity, still we haven't got it fully right. Another reason for that is the fact that we are ever evolving, as new technologies come into existence so are the hacks to counter them. Relationships can mean differently for different people. It could be relationship between two romantic partners, between spouses, between an employee and his boss, between a CEO and his board members, between two

organisations, between two industries, between the president and the citizens. Relationships are nothing but shared understanding between two or more people or between groups.
There is practically no way to decode each and everything about someone however if you consciously choose to give yourself 90 days to let things un-fold without any bias, you will be able to see people as transparently as water.

    i.   You will know whom to Trust whom not to trust
   ii.   Should you extend trust before or ask others to trust you first
  iii.   Who are the people most likely to support you when you fall
  iv.   who might mock you at the very first opportunity
   v.   who will go the extra mile for your cause

and many more insights.... only if you maintained your calm for 90 days and then decided the next course of action.

Yes, Relationships are driven by Trust and Commitments, yet to measure it isn't easy, especially with peoples. The best way to read people is to give them 90 days unbiased but with caution. There will still be few people who may not be subjected to this criterion, but the percentage will be very low. However, for long term benefits, do not judge people for how they look, how they speak, how they present themselves. 90 days gives enough time for you to understand their intent and integrity. The Final conclusions you make about someone shouldn't just be based on what they say but equally based on what you have observed for 90 days. Others foundational principles of Building a relationship are Reciprocity, Compassion, Empathy, Sacrifice, forgiveness, and Truthfulness. All these take turns, as opportunity presents itself during these 90 days. Thus, to have a long and fruitful relationship wherever you are in whoever's company, trust that things will become as transparent as water in just 90 days.

I have seen many people whose views completely changed about me from day 1 to day 90. Initially they had mistaken me as a very agreeable person who will endorse everything as recommended however by the end of 90 days, they realized I am agreeable only if the idea has merit and do not shy away from saying "no" on the face without any remorse.

Stephan M.R Covery in his book The Speed of Trust, gives a unique framework called "Smart Trust Matrix", which is a function of 2 factors propensity to trust and analysis.

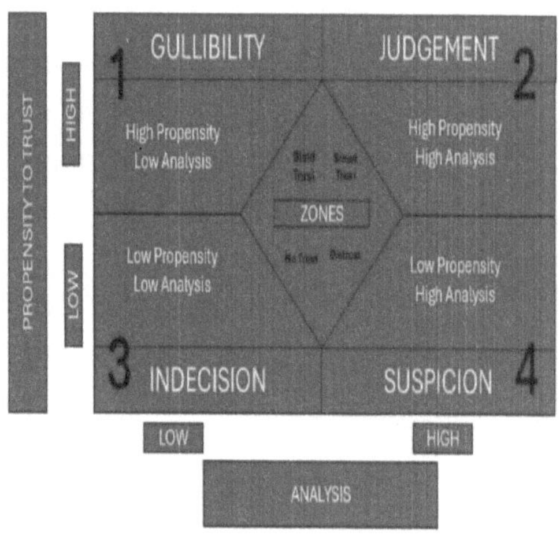

Courtesy Stephan MR Covey "The speed of Trust"

The matrix has 4 zones. Zone 1 has a high propensity of trust and low analysis which leads to a zone of Gullibility or Blind Trust. Zone 2 is High Propensity to Trust and High Analysis;

this is the best zone to be. Zone 3 is Low propensity to Trust and Low Analysis leading to a situation of Indecision and finally zone 4 is suspicion when there is a situation of High analysis and low propensity to Trust.

This matrix gives a good starting point to analyse your current behaviour and make the required behavioural changes to improve interpersonal relationships.

2. Personal Development:

Let me assume you are a Millennials or Gen Y (1981-1996). You are in your mid-career phase; your growth has been plateaued. How can you apply this rule? Even if you belong to any other generation, take a moment and think how can you break through this plateau, facing stagnancy?

90 Day rule suggest that whatever it is that you are interested in, or have set out to achieve, give at least 90 days before quitting and then deciding the next course of action. If you are struck in your career and took up a new course to upskill yourself, give your 100% to the new course. You may feel bored,

face difficulty to grasp the new concepts, may be irritated at times, continue to persist doing what you must. At the end of 90 days, you will have absolute clarity whether to keep paddling or stop, is the course right for you or not. You might wonder if you change your mind, at the end of 90 days pursuing another stream, wasn't your 90 days effort wasted? well not really! Your new pursuit is an outcome of your previous pursuit, it helped you evaluate existing possibilities, aligning it with your core interests and finally providing the next course of actions with most suitable options.

As I reflect, I have seen the power of 90-day rule in my own personal journey across multiple learning initiatives. For most part of my career, I have been into sales and marketing yet kept experimenting with new domain knowledge whenever I could. As a result of which I have built a core expertise across many other fields such as Leadership, Entrepreneurship, Public speaking amongst others. Every 3-6 months I initiate to learn something new with an open mind and the rule of 90 days has been a great enabler thus far. As I write this book, I have started my journey of reading and understanding Sanskrit Language and only time will tell how proficient I become at it.

I do not believe in taking shortcuts and thus do not advocate any such method. You cannot become expert at anything in 15 minutes or a few days. Even if you learnt the craft mentally you need to give your body time to fully internalise it and that will only happen if you let it sink in gradually.

I have spoken about two areas Relationships & Personal Development; however, you can apply this rule in any other situation as you please. You may even try to change your spending habits or adopt an investing habit for first 90 days and the impact of it will be there for everyone to see.

Chapter summary:

1) Rule of 90 days simply means to continue with your endeavours for at least 90 days and then deciding the future course of action.
2) At the end of 90 days, there can be 2 outcomes, either you have developed deep interest in the same field or changed course having realised your initial misalignment.
3) The effort put during the 90 days is never wasted, it is an experiential learning that will come to your aid in future initiatives as well
4) In Relationships, you can apply this rule to understanding the personalities of people around you beyond the initial masks that they may have worn.

5) You can also gauge people's intent towards you and choose the ones you need in your coterie.
6) Keep a close track of your activities, this along with giving insights of what has happened, also preps you for future as well.
7) Time is a most valuable resource, even more valuable than money, learn to maximise every second that you have. First step towards that is recording the current spending methods, only then you can make plans to use it judiciously
8) Every person is unique and thus needs to customize a plan suited as per his own needs and preference. Research says it may take anywhere between 18-254 days to form a habit based on the complexity and individual's environment and motivations.
9) 90-day rule can be applied in any life situation. In Health & wellness, finance & investing, Relationships, work life balance, financial stability and independence, Career and professional growth, Personal development, Travel and lifestyle. The applications are immense.

6. Productivity and Prioritization go hand in hand

"Until we can manage time, we can manage nothing else."

Peter Drucker

How much is too much, and which tasks deserve maximum attention is a conundrum that has kept generations guessing. The Art of Prioritization is a skill that signifies personal mastery. Personal mastery over actions can be achieved by choosing to do what you must, irrespective of your internal state emotionally and external state environmentally.

In the last few chapters, you have discovered that Resilience is the greatest predictor of success. If you have willed it, you will achieve it. During your pursuit you will undoubtedly face setbacks and will continue to march forward taking everything in your stride because you have learnt to reframe all situations positively.

As you proceed you will eventually realize your purpose, the identity, the reason for your existence, which will fire up your engine.

Chapter on "90-day rule" provided insights on sustaining with a method or activity for 90 days then deciding the next course of action, since this allows the situation to become as transparent as water. The 90-day rule coupled with daily activity tracker helps you understand the direction of your actions. At the same time, it removes curtains from a few hidden activities that you are engaged in without your conscious efforts.

This Chapter is about Prioritization, smartly managing the resources you have. Here moderation needs to be exercised. Cooking on a very high flame burns the nutrients, therefore it's important to proceed at an optimal speed and increase or decrease the intensity based on the needs of the situation. Cooked food is the end-product we seek. End-products may vary based on time and the occasion, some food needs to be prepared on a light flame, some on a high flame, some needs to be soaked overnight before cooking. Such are the Goals in life, each goal will require you to prioritize your actions differently based on the resources you have. Sometimes you need to jog, sometimes sprint, or play the waiting game. Your flame is the power you have, to keep pushing. You do not have unlimited flame, you must protect it when it is windy outside, rest when you are exhausted and ensure the same for other resources at your disposal.

On any given day, we have a multitude of things to complete. Even if we have a smaller list, we are not able to complete them fully due to distractions. Many a people are seen sprinting through the office corridors announcing they have too many things on their plate, but the sad reality is, they have a problem prioritizing their tasks. Each task must be approached as per its merit. Merit is based on the categorization you have defined. One of the oldest and widely accepted frameworks for prioritization is Eisenhower Urgent Important Matrix. Two broad Categories of which are Urgent and Important.

The name comes after Dwight D. Eisenhower (1890–1969) who served as the 34th President of the United States from 1953-1961. The matrix was derived from his statement "What is important is seldom urgent, and what is urgent is seldom important". He was known for his Pragmatic Leadership style, Calm demeanour, and strategic approach to problem solving.

The Urgent tasks form the X-axis, and Important tasks form the y-axis. Four possible tasks are urgent and important (DO), Not Urgent and Important (DECIDE),

Urgent but not important (DELEGATE), Not urgent and not important (DELETE).

Every activity will fit in either of the four grids, we just need to categorize the activity and prioritize accordingly.

Table 1:

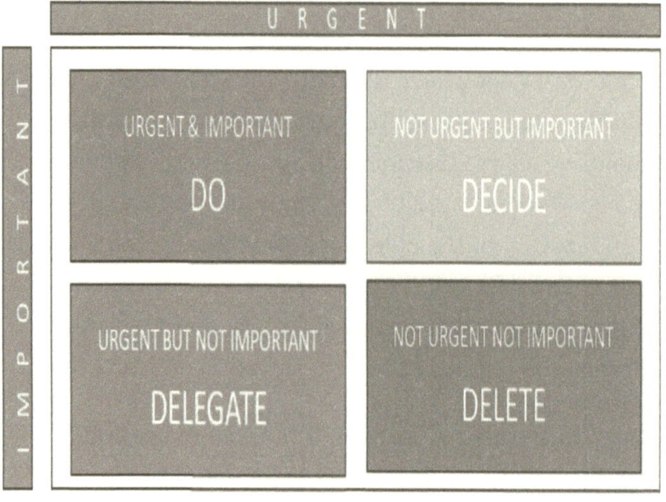

First and foremost, we must understand that everything that is Urgent is not necessarily Important and everything that is Important is not necessarily Urgent. Of course, there will be a few instances where it will hold true, but majority of the time, it is just a categorization problem where we are rushed due to situational pressure.

Let's break down each of the Grids:

1) **Urgent and Important Tasks**: These are the set of tasks that needs to be attended to immediately and cannot be delegated to others. Based on the demographics here are some of the tasks which falls under this head.

Generation (as on 2024)	Urgent and Important Tasks
Silent Generation (1928-1945) [80-97 Years]	Health is of Utmost concern, so getting routine checkups, following prescribed activities for mobility will be on top of the mind.
Baby Boomers (1946-1964) [61-79 years]	Tasks that can provide a peaceful life post-retirement like a good corpus, health cover, securing financial independence, engaging in hobbies will the top priorities
Generation X (1965-1980) [45-60 years]	Career demands, Balancing family commitments, and industry relevant skills will be the top priorities
Millennials (1981-1996) [29-44 years]	Career goals, financial stability, knowledge about new trends will be on top of the activity list

Generation Z (1997-2012) [13-28 years]	Mental health, building new skills, social connections will be on top of the priority list
Generation Alpha (2013-Presnt) [up to 12 years]	Building healthy habits -sleep & nutrition, foundational academic and life skills related tasks

I have given a broad list of tasks that may be relevant based on your group; however, you need to personalize the grid as per your lifestyle, aspirations and resources at your disposal. Urgent and important tasks are crisis situations, deadlines and emergencies. You may have information about the deadlines, but crisis or emergencies can happen any time. To ensure continuity of operations you must deal with these situations urgently. Completing a project presentation for a client meeting, attending to a medical emergency, addressing an urgent staffing issue, handling disputes in the team, resolving discrepancies in financials, last minute request from an authority figure etc.s are all example of Urgent and important tasks.

You must ensure that this quadrant isn't keeping you occupied throughout the day and must keep room for prescheduled things.

2)**Not urgent But Important Tasks**: This is the most important quadrant to focus on. Important tasks are those which contribute to your long-term goals. We discussed the importance of having your own Values, mission and vision statement in the previous chapters. These tasks are the building blocks of the future goals that you have.

Here you must Decide, that means make a list of activities that is contributing to your long-term goals. Then schedule a time during the day or week which is dedicated to each of these activities. You can either have fixed time blocked each day or keep a moving schedule to achieve the defined target hours anytime throughout the day. For e.g. If you have a long-term goal of becoming a data scientist, you can allocate 2 hours of coding practice every evening 10-12 pm before bed or keep it moving anytime during the day at a stretch or short intervals whenever opportunity presents. Likewise for other goals that you may have.

Let me give a personal example: As I realised the purpose of my life: to share what I know, with the intent to empower people so they become the best version of themselves. I started investing a fixed amount of time most days after 9-5 work to upgrade my knowledge on multiple fronts. One such front was Motivational speaking; I wanted to speak with impact, anytime opportunity presented itself. I knew this wasn't an easy field to master. Most people have spent years together and still haven't achieved a reasonable ground in the field of motivational public speaking.

This was one of my "Important but not urgent activity". Most people, to achieve something like this, would take a course from a reputed institute, spending lakhs or join some club where they can pick the tricks of the trade. I am not discounting those methods. Yet I followed a slightly different approach, my curiosity to learn new things has always presented me with new perspectives to every situation. I started improving my vocabulary by reading good books and speeches of famous personalities. Started including those keywords, phrases in day-to-day conversations in professional setting. Since I was part of executive committee professionally, I could notice the techniques of other Leaders and tie it back to everything I was learning. Eventually I built upon the structure and methods to create a hook in each talk, alongside other intricacies. For me every situation was an opportunity to exercise what I was learning. I could see the differences in ways people addressed me before and then after a year. The investment that I had made wasn't a lot, yet it was continuous.

Finally, I Joined a local speaking club, tested my public speaking skills in a diverse group of audience. That accelerated the entire process; in just 3 months of time, I exceeded my expectations amongst a group of people, who have been mastering the craft from decades. I gave my first motivational talk in front of 150+ people from all walks of life in the age group of 20- 65 years and it was fabulous. It was the first major Validation that my method was simple yet very effective.

I achieved an outcome in just 1.5 years that many couldn't achieve in decades courtesy to small consistent efforts and a method so simple that most people find boring to adopt. I have followed a similar method for other important tasks as well. Some are already completed; some are in the process. Similarly, you may have goals that are not urgent but are important, it could be re-designing your career trajectory, earning X amount of money, or any other objective. You can follow this method to achieve the goals in one tenth of the time taken by other people.

You must work towards making the 2nd Quadrant biggest of all quadrants. This is because you are preparing to do what will be required in the future. The ability to foresee and plan the actions in present context, is the greatest differentiator between a Leader and a manager. Aim to Become a Leader, not a manager.

3)**Urgent But Not-Important Tasks**: These are those tasks that must ideally be Delegated to others or delayed. There may or may not be anyone who can do it with same finesse but if someone can do it with even 80% effectiveness, give them an opportunity. This quadrant unnecessarily inflates the list of activities that you have, and you feel overwhelmed.

You may get multiple requests for attending conferences, webinars, doing a favour etc., but not all of them are important for you, it might just be a courtesy request. You can always assign someone to attend on your behalf in cases like that. Similarly, as you start your day, you don't necessarily have to reply to tens of emails as the first activity of the day, you can choose to respond to a select few and forward the rest to your colleague for the next steps.

Just take a pause as the work presents itself and decide if that needs your immediate attention or can be delayed. A big chuck of our everyday tasks is amongst those which need to be just pushed for a later point in time.

If you expand your quadrant 2 of not urgent but important tasks, it will also reduce the number of activities from quadrant 3, since your efficiency of doing things has become better due to consistent efforts towards the activity.

Simply put, you can either delay or delegate the tasks as per its merit.

4)**Not Urgent Not Important tasks**: These are pure time wasters and must be deleted immediately. These make up a good chuck of everyday routine. Social media and blue screens are the most common ways of wasting time.

Today on average millennial and Gen-Z operate anywhere between 2-4 electronic devices like laptop, mobile phone, Television set etc., switching between each of them repeatedly as per their likings. The blue screen usage can vary between 2.5-5 hours between different user groups.

Similarly gossiping, Unproductive meetings, Overthinking, are all other pure timewasters that must be eliminated.

Eisenhower's matrix can be applied by individuals and organizations alike. I have personally seen organizations having pasted this simple chart in their departmental offices to increase the productivity of their employees. Personally, whenever something presents itself out of the blue I try and categorize it as per the matrix and determine the intervention that is needed.

Self-Discipline is closely interlinked to productivity management. How consistent you are with your efforts will determine how good you become. With consistency comes efficiency, which gives better control over time.

Self-Discipline:

Self-Discipline is your ability to control your emotions and actions in any situation, by virtue of your choice and not feelings. You getting failed at everything you do is life pushing you, you can either push it back or accept the failure as is. Self-Discipline empowers you to stay committed to the cause despite the setbacks.

The difference between thriving and surviving is self-discipline...
The difference between reaching goals and falling short is self-discipline...
The gap between achieving dreams and giving up is self-discipline...
The difference between a rich and poor is self-discipline...
The difference between dreams and reality is self-discipline...
In short Self-Discipline is the Engine that drives personal growth and success...

Self-Discipline comes with self-control. Self-control means to always keep your emotions in check. It also includes staying calm and composed in challenging situations, and not letting emotions dictate actions. You must aim to resist the temptation to act on immediate desires in favour of long-term goals for e.g. If you want to become fit & healthy, you need to choose a nutritious food over fast food, even when you are craving something unhealthy in consideration of the long-term health goals. If you are building a financial discipline, then you need to stick to a budget and save money instead of making impulsive purchases. Similarly, you need to exercise self-control in other areas of your life as well.

As discussed in chapter 1, to build resilience as a skill it is important to self-reflect as often as possible. Journaling, meditation and asking questions to self are some of the most powerful ways to build resilience. As it turns out, the more you self-reflect the more aware you become of your internal state, having an awareness of your internal state you are empowered to manage yourself better. If you can do this consistently you are also building your self-discipline routine. You may notice that Self-reflection is at center of acquiring most skills in life, managing self and managing others likewise.

Journaling is the most underrated method today. Although there has been an increased adoption of journaling geographically, many give it up too soon after a few days. One common reason for this is the fact that "thinking is difficult". No one likes to think, yet everyone likes to dream big. Both have their own significance. In the upcoming chapters we will also talk about visualization and how that leads to better successful outcomes. Before that let us understand the importance of self-reflecting. Upon re-visiting past experiences at the end of the day consistently you become emotionally stronger, calmer, more focused and clearer in your outlook.

We do not learn from experiences; we learn by reflecting on those experiences and Journaling is the best way to learn from our experiences.

Our Proclivity to digital gadgets is another reason why we don't invest time journaling these days. There are far too many choices, and we have been spoilt due to that. When was the last time you took a pen and a diary and tried to write down your experience for that day or any other persistent thought troubling you. It is a rarity today, having shifted our focus from traditional tools to digital tools. Writing and reading digitally has become a norm, however I still feel the most creative ideas come when you take a pen and paper and let your thoughts flow spatially.

Coming Back to the chapter theme, Productivity isn't just how many things you can do effectively or how fast you can do multiple things. It also means not to indulge in activities which are timewasters and managing personal self, better by being more self-aware, being more self-disciplined.

Mobile usage is another critical area that needs to be attended to Improve productivity. Imagine you are working on an important project and suddenly the phone beeps. What do you do? If you restrained from responding to that specific call or text notification it would be somewhat okay, however you get carried away doing other things on the phone thereafter Jumping to different social media applications. Discovering notifications has become an epidemic now. We are constantly seeking notification, and the social media companies understand this very well.

Has it ever happened, when you opened your social profiles after a gap of 2-3 days there were zero notifications. Well, I don't think so. You always have something in your feed. If not from your social connections, then from the social network itself. They are all craving for your attention and billions of dollars are spent each year to grab that attention of yours for a host of products or services out there. Do you need those products: maybe or maybe not, but the sheer volume of advertisements that are thrown at you is mind-boggling. We have learned to look the other way and occasionally click a few times here and there. And on those few occasions that we click there exists a digital war amongst the companies to grab your click. Mind you, social networks are not just limited to being the facilitator, they have become creators as well. With AI in the fold, content generation, promotion and iterations are happening at a speed unlike any time before. And even before you figure out your likes and dislikes, digital agencies have made an infallible method to keep you hooked based on your past browsing history, engagements with articles or video shorts.

And then we wonder:

why aren't we productive?
Why do we get distracted so easily?
Why aren't we efficient?

Research[2] says that an average person interacts with their smartphones more than 1000 times per day encompassing touch, swipe, clicks etc. The number may vary from region to region, but the range is once every 2 mins to once every 10 mins. Smartphones have become an integral part of our lifestyle in the way to conduct ourselves. Here the most important question we must ask ourselves is, can we keep some distance from our phones and optimize our schedule?

Here are some real-life scenarios where the use of mobile phones can be minimized:

1) While attending scheduled meetings:

   Meetings which are already planned require your full attention and must be distraction free as much as possible. While in the meeting, keep your mobiles in "do not disturb" mode away from your eyesight. If you need to keep it on, then consider keeping it face down and in silent mode, so unnecessary notifications do not break your attention. Often, I have seen people responding to calls & text in the middle of crucial meetings, and sometimes these people are the ones who are leading the meeting. While you are attending a group meeting as a host or a participant, you must aim to give complete attention to the agenda at hand. This will save your time post meeting when others are re-clarifying discussion points, unsure what actions to take, you can march ahead with confidence and complete the deliverables. While having a dialogue with someone, avoid keeping phones on the table or holding them in hand. This distracts the other person since they feel you are not totally present in the moment and not paying full attention to whatever they have to say. This does not just lead to low-trust situations but also creates a transactional relationship over time, if the same behaviour is demonstrated. You are bound to get distracted and distract the other person as long as you keep fidgeting with your mobile phone. The quality of your social interactions and personal interactions can be significantly improved by reducing your interactions with the mobile phone.

2) First thing when you get up from sleep:

The first thing when you get up is the best time to structure your thoughts which decides the direction of your actions and if that is wasted scrolling mobile phone with unstructured content, the mind is confused. Avoid touching the mobile phone as you get up or restrict to just checking the time if you have the habit of sleeping with the mobile phone.

3) While attending to nature's call

There is an increasing trend where a lot of teens and adults like to carry their mobile phones inside the washroom when they go for bowel emptying. As per some estimates[3,4] more than 50% of adults have admitted to using their mobile phones in the washroom and more than 80% of the teens reportedly use mobiles in the washrooms.

4) During Meals

This is common across all age groups and people tend to engage in some or the other content consumption as they eat. This shifts the focus from the food to the media played on the screen, reducing the appeal of the dish. The aroma, appearance, texture, taste is not fully relished since the concentration is shifted. We often tend to eat more as we are glued to screen, chewing less, leading to a poor digestion process.

These are the few instances where you can start to minimize the use of mobile phones to be in better control of your schedule. Aim to have a clear space wherever you study or work, keep it organized. Your external environment also impacts your productivity like the space, type of people, temperature and other intricacies. The art of prioritization lies in effectively managing both your internal as well as external state.

Chapter summary:

1) The Art of Prioritization is a skill that signify personal mastery. Personal mastery over actions can be achieved by choosing to do what you must, irrespective of your internal state emotionally and external state environmentally.
2) You do not have unlimited flame, you must protect it when it is windy outside, rest when you are exhausted and ensure the same for other resources at your disposal.
3) Each task must be approached as per its merit.
4) One of the oldest and widely accepted frameworks for prioritisation is Eisenhower Urgent Important Matrix. Two broad Categories of which are Urgent and Important.
5) Do the urgent and important tasks, Decide or Schedule the not urgent but important tasks, Delegate the not important but urgent tasks and finally Delete the not important not urgent tasks.
6) Self-Discipline is closely interlinked to productivity. Since with consistency comes efficiency in the tasks.
7) Self-Discipline comes with self-control. Self-control means to always keep your emotions in

check. It also includes staying calm and composed in challenging situations, and not letting emotions dictate actions.

8) Journaling, Meditating and asking questions to self are some of the best ways to practice self-reflection

9) Mobile usage is a critical area that needs to be attended to Improve productivity. Aim to have technology work for you and not the other way round.

7. Drive your Motivation

"The biggest secret of life is that there is no secret. Whatever your goal, you can get there if you are willing to work."

Oprah Winfrey

Motivation is what keeps you going in your pursuit of success. Motivation can be internal or external. Internal when it stems from your own core beliefs and ideology, external when you seek the inspiration from the outside world, from people or environments.

I started going to gym at the age of 18 while I was in my boarding school at Dehradun. The only time I have taken a longer break (more than 30 days) has been 3 instances so far in the last 16 years. First during my 12th Board exams, second during my IIT-JEE Coaching and third is now to complete this book. For the rest of the period, I have always found time, no matter how occupied I was.

As I have grown, I have continued to Exercise yet the motivation behind it has kept changing. In my teens I was motivated because I wanted to be the strongest person in my class. As a young adult it was to have an attractive personality, and now as an adult it is for the boost of Dopamine, the feel-good factor along with a healthy mind free of stress and worries. If I got into an argument with a colleague, or did not perform a task as per my satisfaction, or faced an unfavourable situation, it affected my mood and the best way to come out those emotional states has been exercising over the years.

Motivation is dynamic and changes with time. We are living in a fast-paced world and are bound to be influenced by the changes happening around us. The number of choices has increased multiple times, and every choice leads to a different experience and each experience leads to a specific outcome which in turn will impact on the level of motivation we have.

At the end of it all, it all boils down to the choices we make. Making choices is the easiest thing to do, but making the right choices is most difficult. Today the attention span has reduced to just 8 seconds as per research conducted by Microsoft[1], which was earlier used to be around 12 seconds till the year 2000. This means there is a possibility that something will drive away our attention every 10 seconds. It becomes critical not to get distracted. Thus, making the right choices without getting distracted is the habit which keeps us motivated.

Find your reasons, Reasons behind the choices you make and choose better every new moment. This is the simplest hack you can apply to stay motivated.

Motivation and Results:

What would you say about the startup ecosystem which is up on the rise in the last few years post the covid-19 pandemic.

In India alone, there has been close to 117,000 new startups[2] registered post the pandemic and it has been on the rise ever since in most of the states. There is another shocking stat which says that close to 70-90% of all startups fail during the first 5 years of starting. Only 5-10% of startups[4] go on to become profitable. Imagine If the success of an organization is measured in terms of the revenue it generates and it has failed to do that in last couple of years. How could someone stay motivated during those periods. Results must be broken down to smaller milestones as much as possible. This serves as check post as one progresses and provides an opportunity to course correct should there be a need. Milestones broken down into smaller time frames make the goal more realistic no matter how aspirational it may be.

Companies like Netflix, Apple, Amazon and a few others struggled a lot in their initial 5 years however kept iterating, entering new markets. They kept learning and improving themselves before finally making a big impact on the masses. The risk-taking appetite can be different for different people but is closely linked to the internal motivation state. You may not be clocking the forecasted revenues as a business owner or in any other capacity, however your persistence to keep going is dependent on how motivated you are with each failure.

Daniel Kahneman and Amos Tversky[3] in their 1979 paper on Prospect theory: An analysis of Decision under risk" Demonstrated that people tend to avoid risks when facing potential gains and prefer risks when trying to avoid losses. Daniel Kahneman elaborated on this theory in further detail in his book "Thinking fast and slow".

Only if we can take more risks when there is a potential to make greater gains, can the performance of the startup ecosystem be improved in the times to come.

Some people face Crucible moments in their journey. Crucible moments are those which impact life. These are life altering moments like loss of someone, loss of job, a permanent disability, market crash or anything else that affects them very deeply. These moments continue to serve as motivation in all moments. In moments of relaxation, sleep, indulgence or wastages of time, these serve as reminders to keep pushing, stay motivated and chart the course.

Can Motivation be created?

What do you do when you want to become a musician or a singer? You go and attend live performances digitally or in person of your favourite artist. This is done to seek inspiration, with inspiration flows motivation, with motivation actions which lead to the results. After you have attended the live performances, the memory stays afresh in the mind, like where you sat in the crowd, new conversations with likeminded people, or a selfie moment with the stage performer if you were lucky. This strengthens your resolve further towards becoming a musician yourself. But soon after a few days, the sharpness of the event gets clouded with other routine chores, and motivation dwindles.

Here efforts need to be directed towards integrating these events into your lifestyle, so it serves as a constant reminder, adding fuel to the fire. The idea is to imprint the event's positive memory on both conscious and subconscious self, making the required behaviour automatic in everyday schedule. Consider changing the wallpaper background of the mobile phone or your computer screen. Consider following the artist on social media to stay tuned to all his/her posts. Read more about the artist. Paste a note on your study table/working table. You can do a multitude of things to revisit the event as much as possible to seek inspiration. The human mind needs to be reminded multiple times, to internalize any memory consciously as well as subconsciously. In the earlier chapters we spoke about the number of days it takes to make a behaviour automatic, in which research concludes varying number of days, ranging between 18-254 days based on the individual and the habit.

Here, in the context of seeking motivation, the memory of the event must be repeated as many times as possible by varying number of methods, print, digitally and mentally (by reflection).

I recently attended a Literature festival in Bengaluru, where I met an author, whose books had a profound impact on how I spent or saved money. "Let's talk money" & "Let's talk mutual funds" are two books which have given me enough knowledge to intelligently manage money for the next couple of years without being worried. The sad reality is that financial literacy isn't taught in schools and colleges in a systematic way and thus many people still do not know what to do with their money. I was always motivated to invest money but did not know the right methods of investing and these 2 books gave me enough insights to get started and build upon that. After about 1 month of reading the book I met Monika Halan, took a selfie with her and shared the impact that her book had on me. I also changed the wallpaper of my computer and mobile screen (with that selfie) to revisit the moment multiple times to stay on course of building an investing disciple. It's been a few months since then but my motivation to invest right has been on the rise.

Even after I have learnt the concepts of financial literacy, I am still feeding my subconscious to apply the learnt principle every time I look at the picture with the author. This ensures my motivation to follow a discipline to investing does not go haywire. I pasted a "sticky note" in front of my study table which says: "investing is continuous, not one time activity" so I don't invest everything in one month and do nothing in the subsequent months.

By smartly revisiting past experiences from your memory, you can create anchors of motivation, Whenever and wherever you need.

What are anchors?

Anchors could be anything that helps you course correct on a path that you want to follow but have veered away due to a controllable or an uncontrollable stimulus. For example: Everyone wants to read good books, but most get veered away scrolling through social media feeds. Scrolling feeds are a controllable stimulus however, if someone is struck with power outage then it is an uncontrollable stimulus.

Anchors could be a tangible object or intangible idea or a certain way of synchronising body and mind that helps bring your attention to the task at hand and succeed at it. It could also be a certain belief that you have formulated to come to your rescue whenever you are diverted. Let me explain this with an analogy. Whenever you call upon God, you close your eyes recite few specific words to pay respect and seek blessings. In Hindu shastras every God has a specific mantra which is recited to pay respect and seek their blessings. Whenever you say those specific words, you bring you attention to God and nothing else, you are fully immersed into the moment, seeking their blessings. Similarly, you can also frame specific words which when repeated mentally can bring you out of a depressing situation, provide confidence, and control anger (can be used to in any situation). In terms of Objects, it can be a photograph, a card, ring, coin or anything else that re-aligns your thought, bringing you back on track negating the diversion. In other words, this is known as neuro linguistic programming. A method of programming the brain to behave in a certain way in any situation. NLP has far wide applications in therapy and counselling, sports and performance, personal management, relationships and other fields.

If you are feeling extremely nervous before giving a presentation, you can create a mental anchor of a few words, something like this: "Giving presentations excites me and this is another opportunity to showcase my skills". Imagine yourself repeating this line mentally couple of times and now introspect what is better, using this anchor to excel at the task of presentation or being worried about the stage fear. Clearly this will give you more confidence and the motivation to win over your audience.

Having portraits of famous personalities hung on the walls, also serves as an inspiration as you are constantly reminded of the feats of their achievements, the struggles they have endured and how can you, from position of disadvantage reach the height of success by emulating some of their traits. You have seen many walls decorated with powerful quotes to inspire the onlookers, however you may or may not have been inspired by them but take a pause here and think for a moment! *"Can I design my external environment with similar quotes, pictures of personalities who have greatly inspired me"*

You are the master of your internal as well as external environment. You can choose what needs to be impressed upon your memory, how frequently and why. If you can curate this experience for yourself your motivation level will unquestionably rise.

Personally, I carry the passport size picture of Swami Vivekananda in my wallet from last couple of years. This is a visual anchor which I have created to motivate myself towards my learning initiatives. Swami Vivekananda achieved so much in his short life span of 39 years that most people haven't in their entire lifetime. He founded Ramakrishna Mission in 1897 which has gone from strength to strength even today and is a testament to his commitment towards service to humanity & empowerment for all. He believed that education could eradicate poverty, inequality, and ignorance which are the same values I realise are needed to succeed in modern world as well. Even though necessities of food and shelter is mostly met however quality education for all is still a far cry that needs to be addressed. There is an increased accessibility to education across the demographic however it is not producing people with core fundamental values towards humanity and that is a gap which require an out of the box perspective to address.

I continue to seek motivation from swami Vivekananda since his mission is aligned with my current values to empower people to become the best version of themselves. Similarly, you can also create a visual anchor who greatly inspire you.

This is a personal example of motivation by Emulation. Emulate someone so it becomes second nature. It is easier to set goals but very difficult to formulate a system to achieve those goals. Emulating someone reduces the cognitive load to create new ideas, ideate, prototype and then scale. Here, what becomes important is the person you emulate. You are temporarily asking someone else to drive your ship and moments like this require a significant "leap of faith". Even though that person is not present with you, you are letting their thoughts, beliefs, and doings become your guide to navigate an unfamiliar path which could have taken more time otherwise.

Motivation and Purpose:

Motivation to do what you must stems from the purpose that you have. Purpose comes first motivation follows. Purpose helps you find your true calling, the reason for your existence. What would you do today if you were to die tomorrow. Having a clearly defined purpose is like solving half the problem even before starting It. There is a famous saying if you have six hours to chop a tree, spend four sharpening the axe. With so many man-made tools of distraction around, keeping oneself motivated has become a herculean task. This is why skills like Resilience, positive reframing, rule of 90 days needed to be considered to keep the focus on the task at hand.

As per Hindu shastras there are four Purusharthas (4 goals of human life)

1. Dharma (righteousness, duty): this means to follow one's moral duty towards self, others, ancestors, society and the nature. This forms the foundation for all the other Purusharthas and provides the basis for right way of living. It also means to live in harmony with all.
2. Arth (meaning of life): It signifies the pursuit of materialistic pleasures, wealth, prosperity needed to live a comfortable life.
3. Kaam (pleasures): it signifies achievement of sensual pleasure, mental and emotional well-being without violating dharma (moral well-being) and Arth (material well-being)
4. Moksha (Liberation): Signifies liberation and spiritual well-being. It also means to achieve a state of self-actualisation.

One's motivation can stem from any of all the four Purusharthas. It is important to realize the purpose of life and stay motivated to pursue it even in the face of difficulties.

Chapter Summary:

1. Motivation is dynamic and changes with time, as our interest, beliefs and external environment change. It's important to find the right source of motivation.
2. Choices can impact the motivation state, so aim to make smart choices. At the same time try to understand the reasons behind those choices.
3. Results are not in your control but making a choice to stay motivated is very much controllable with the right tools
4. Your risk appetite can have a say on your motivation state. Most people are risk averse that is why a radical change is rarely seen. Understand that a greater risk has the potential to demotivate you but also increase the threshold of taking on new tasks without getting demotivated.
5. Results are not directly proportional to the level of efforts. It is different for different individuals. Fail often to succeed faster.
6. Motivation can be created with the help of anchors which can change the mental and emotional state of being. Anchors can be tangible objects or phrases that can be exercised upon during a time of need.
7. An event that motivates you can be revisited upon multiple times by means of self-reflection.
8. NLP has proven to a powerful technique to increase motivational state by reframing and labelling.

9. You can design your external environment to continuously seek motivation by quotes, pictures or messages that inspire you.
10. Motivational levers must also be impressed upon the subconscious memory, so it becomes a second nature.
11. There are 4 Purusharthas as per Hindu shastras or four goals of life, Dharm (morality), Arth (materialistic well-being), Kaam (Love, Pleasure), Moksha (Liberation). Either of it can be taken as a source of motivation to keep going.

8. Visualisation and Affirmations

"As you think, so shall you become."

Bruce Lee

US Navy seals undergo a 6-week training that also includes one week popularly known as "Hell week" where they get only 4 hours of sleep over a 60-hour period while being wet most of the time. Even after carefully selecting the best of the individuals more than 75% (75 out of 100) of the candidates drop out during this 6- week program. It was concluded that it couldn't just be the IQ or physical attributes since these selected people were amongst the best in terms of IQ and physical traits.

Eric Potterat[1] a renowned psychologist was hired to remedy this situation, and he came up with the "Big 4 framework" which led to a significant improvement in the number of candidates who cleared the training.

Big 4 frameworks:

1. Focus on the right now:

    while we are in the middle of something, we let other thoughts creep in and derail our focus. This habit advises to stay focused on the immediate short-term goal.

2. Imagine how good it will feel:

    How do you feel when you have tasted victory? Or achieve a milestone? That is one very strong positive feeling. Imagine you have already reached that winning mark if running, completed a deadline or achieved any other outcome while you were just starting.

3. When all fails, Breathe deeply:

    whenever you start to feel "I can't do it", "I am failing", "I may not make it", the amygdala in the brain gets activated towards the survival mode. To change this mental state, we must influx the blood with oxygen to calm down the Amygdala. Eric potterat recommends breathing in 6 2 6 methods. 6 seconds of deep inhalation to fill the lungs completely with oxygen, 2 seconds pause and again 6 seconds of exhalation just 3 times anytime during the day. This can lead to reduced blood pressure and improved decision making

4. Cheer yourself on:

What is the mental voice telling you, program your mind to cheer you up as you progress with words like, "I can do it", "I have excelled at far bigger tasks", "I was waiting for this opportunity" so on and so forth.
Pessimism is a major cause of failure for most individuals. Thoughts like I haven't had a good sleep, I lack few technical skills, I haven't prepared well etc are negative pessimistic talks that should be avoided at all costs.

Using these 4 methods US Navy Seals were able to crack one of the toughest trainings on this planet so people like you and me can easily achieve tasks of lesser difficulty with greater ease.

Why should you Visualize?

There is a famous saying, "To foresee is to rule" yet very few can. Visualization as a tool helps train your mind to become expectant for what is about to come in harmony with internal values and beliefs. Visualization is an open canvas that helps you paint a picture in a way that you desire, you are the protagonist and everyone else are support cast. It expands the horizon of the mind thinking beyond the normal scripts that are handed to you by friends, family, societies, and institutions. Most of the time you are given a standard operating procedure to adhere to as soon as you take on a task, which indirectly defines a boundary that you cannot cross.

Visualization knows no boundary, almost anything is possible to visualize. It's the way of the mind. Dr Stephan R Covey[2] in his book "The 7 habits of highly effective people" speaks about a concept called: All things are created twice, first is the mental creation and second is the physical creation. All Ideas are first cooked upon in the minds incubator and then acted upon in the physical realm.

Napolean Hill[3], in his book Think and grow rich quotes, "whatever the mind can conceive and believe, it can achieve". Many other renowned authors have credited visualization as a robust tool to achieve greatness in life.

The Research says that Brain cannot differentiate between what is already true and what is fiction. Thus, by means of continuous affirmations brains start to believe you already possess what you crave and change the mindset accordingly. This changed mindset starts to transmute into actions and actions eventually lead to results that you had been craving.

Earlier this used to be a trade secret practiced by very few, but more and more people across different disciplines are practicing the techniques of visualization to excel at their field now. Many Leading sportspersons have become a keen practitioner now replaying the kind of performance they want to demonstrate on the game day, be it cricket, football, swimming or any other sport. This gives the confidence to take on the toughest of opponents having already won the battle mentally.

Jim Carey[4] a Canadian American actor known for his hit performances in Ace Ventura, Pet Detective, The Mask, Visualized writing himself a cheque for $10 Million dollar for "acting services rendered" and dated in 10 years in the future in the year 1985. Just before thanksgiving in year 1995 he was chosen to cast in the movie "Dumb and Dumber" for a fee of $10 million dollars. Arnold Schwarzenegger is also a big believer of visualization and has been practicing this technique in both acting and politics and has been very vocal about it.

As per study [5] it was found that mental rehearsal (or visualization) is powerful because the subconscious processes the experience as a real one (by firing those neurons that are responsible for skill acquisition). It makes the person calmer and more adapted to stressful situations and can speed up the learning process as well.

Take Command of your life

We all follow a script, a script that we have crafted knowingly and unknowingly, but mostly unknowingly. As we give in to the circumstances and let desires dictate actions we gradually gravitate towards a life of comfort and relaxation. Not that one should not crave the luxuries of life, but the point I am trying to make is one shouldn't get habituated with that. Visualization enables one to take a pause and think beyond. If you don't pause to think about the future, past experiences keep playing in the mind, in which you are iterating how you could have performed better, did something else to prove supremacy. Pause to think ahead and do that in present tense always.

When you tell your brain you are running a successful company with 1000 employees spread over 5 branches, your brain starts to believe it as true and starts looking for answers in everyday affairs. You have planted a seed in your brain which needs nourishment to grow, and this nourishment is received by the power of observation. Just this time your observation power has multiplied manifolds having visualized an outcome already. The moment you see or hear another entrepreneur running a successful company you immediately start to resonate with him and imbibe his traits subconsciously. You mirror and match him in your day-to-day affairs. All of this starts with one visualization, you tend to break old unproductive habits, form new stronger habits become better than your older version in no time.

You decide your path and are not dependent on the scripts handed out to you. You have the power to change the scripts by the power of visualization. Mentally rehearse where you would see yourself in the next five, ten, fifteen years and adopt that mindset today by a conscious choice.

Visualization must be done by impressing the events upon all five senses of touch, taste, auditory, sight, smell. Amongst the five senses majority of people are mostly visual, auditory and kinaesthetic type. Those who are inclined towards picture and images are known to have visual personalities, those towards sounds as auditory, those towards touch and feel as kinaesthetic.

Going back to the previous example of running a company with 1000 employees having five branches, now also visualize the intersection at which the office is located, the colour of the building, the arrangement of the chairs, the décor inside, arrangement of lightening, you corner cabin, the family pic on the desk , your credentials on the walls, the cushioning of your chair. After you have scripted the visuals then feel the Leather and Texture of the office sofa set, touch and feel the photograph of your family that you have hung on the walls, enjoy a cup a coffee from the vending machine.

How does it taste? Go deeper and deeper into the mental imagery and let your emotions flow. As you progress, go crafting minutest of the detail and let the experience get recorded in the mind's eye.

Today there are more consumers than creators. Take for example social media platforms like LinkedIn, as per article [6] only 1% of the total users from a base of 900 million, create weekly content and the rest 899 million users are all consumers. Amongst those 1% it needs to be determined what percentage are original creators verses the deliverers. However, creating anything requires the application of visualization, to construct the story in a way that will be accepted by the social audience. Writing blogs, recording videos, journaling taps into the creative brain expanding the horizon of imagination. You must aim to create your own footprints as a creator not as a consumer. Create not just for the social platform but the way of life that you aspire to have.

Visualize with Morality:

Just because you can create and run any mental movie and feel it emotionally doesn't mean you should. There should always be some boundary that must be followed. Here the most important boundary that must never be forgotten is Ethics and Morality. As you grow, your road to success must be driven by a mindset of interdependence, doing the right thing for people. Enabling and empowering all those you can in whichever little capacity possible. Visualize with the right intent to create first and seek later, provide first and relish later, become the creator first then the consumer. All of this without compromising your morality. If your peer happens to outperform you in any of the disciples do not become defensive, rather seek to take inspiration from him and let this inspiration feed your aspiration of improvising on that skill. The point is: it cannot start with jealousy, hatred and animosity. Every religion has a different way of saying the Golden rule, a universal concept that should be imbibed by all.

Christianity: "So in everything, do to others what you would have them do to you"

Islam: "None of you truly believes until he loves for his brother what he loves for himself"

Judaism: "What is hateful to you, do not do to your neighbour. This is the whole Torah; the rest is the explanation"

Hinduism: "This is the sum of duty: Do nothing to others which would cause you pain if done to you"

Buddhism: "Hurt not others in ways that you yourself would find hurtful"

Confucianism: "Do not do to others what you do not want done to yourself"

Sikhism: "Treat others as you would be treated yourself"

Jainism: "One should treat all beings as he himself would be treated"

Zoroastrianism: "That nature alone is good which refrains from doing unto another whatsoever is not good for itself"

It's important to practice morality not just while visualization but also in ways we conduct ourselves day in day out. Living a life with morality, integrity and a genuine sense of care and compassion is one that is appreciated by all religions.

Power of Affirmation and Visualization:

As you continue to impress upon your mental faculties, it's also important to do this on a recurring basis and here affirmations play a key role. Affirmations are carefully curated phrases which when repeated consciously get internalized into the subconscious mind. Affirmations are proven to reprogram the belief system over a period when practiced continuously.

If there was a magic pill proven to show result in just few seconds of taking it, it is Affirmations. Affirmations are a successor to visualization. Visualization gives shape to your aspirations which when coupled with affirmations increases the overall effectiveness of the method. Affirmations are like smaller messages which keep solidifying the version that we aspire to be. Affirmations bring tangibility to the visual picture that we have created.

I remember an instance when I had to give a presentation at Century Club Bangalore to healthcare professionals from across the state. I have given multiple talks to IT Professionals but not many to senior healthcare professionals. I was feeling a little more tense than usual. Healthcare professions are amongst the very learned community and invest a significant amount of their time studying and sharpening their craft till the time they retire and few even after that. Here I was about to give a major talk, and the negative voices started to clutter my mind, my blood pressure and heartbeat went up and I could feel the rush of adrenaline. I was neatly dressed in a suit and looked impeccable, yet the stress started to build inside. To calm my mind, I took a sip of cold coffee, yet it wasn't of much help, and finally my name was called! Let's welcome Mr. Ajay with a huge round of applause!

I connected the laptop with the projector on the table in an open house setting and opened the slides to present. Just as I was about to start, I saw many curious eyes glued to me, waiting for what I was about to say. The noises became louder in my head, "I won't be able to give a confident talk", "I am not well prepared", "I am feeling nervous" and other similar thoughts shackled me.

I took the mike and spoke the following words next, "Good evening, I am honoured to be Present here amongst all of you, from such esteemed institutions across Karnataka". While I said this, I realized the hand mike position wasn't perfect and only half the sentence was transmitted from mike, anxiously I repeated the same line re-adjusting the position of mike. Yet this time the voice came with a little tremor. This almost unsettled me on the stage, and I became even more conscious of the eyes staring at me. It was at this moment I exercised my resilience and positive self-talk and said to myself, I cannot fail, I have spoken at much larger forums (in my visualization) with greater ease, took a deep breath (habit 3 of big 4 framework given my Eric potterat) and continued ahead and to my surprise it went very smoothly after that. I moved on stage with greater confidence and conquered my stage freight in a matter of minutes. I am certain it would not have been possible if I hadn't been practicing visualization and affirmation for the last couple of months. It was at this point that I realized the true power of affirmation and visualization, winning from a point where most people would give up.

I must disclose, my method wasn't just limited to practicing visualization alone, I have slogged myself to learn the skills. One of my core principles is to do things which are hard to copy. I prepare myself extensively for weeks, months and years based on the goal and complement it with tools like visualization and affirmations. I do not encourage daydreaming as a solution to all your problems, I am advocating burning the midnight oil but at the same time practice visualizations and affirmations to accelerate the process.

There have been various other incidents where I just visualize how the events would unfold, which gives me the confidence to perform as per my expectation making the mental imagery near reality.

Here are 3 simple ways to practice visualization and affirmation:

1. Create your own scripts for life:

    Just like how a director crafts each scene in a movie, you are the director and actor of your own life. Your parents, relatives, employers are equivalent to the producers of a movie who provide you resources to support your aspirations. However, as you grow you must realise you are your own back up. So, plant seeds that grow into trees by giving you results in due course when you need them, Visualisation is just like a seed which takes time and nourishment to show results. Your conviction and beliefs are the nourishment it needs. Even the world's best coach cannot teach you anything unless you made a choice to believe in her teachings. Sometimes you can take a leap of faith and believe based on the past success of the method you are about to adopt, and it starts giving you the results. Sometimes you look at others to seek validation and approval. In either case unless you believe it will not show the results. As you create your own scripts either in the mental screen or in a notebook, give it your undoubted belief that it will come true. The time to show results can be different for different individuals, since it based on a host of other parameters as well and it is not just visualisation that brings results, but visualisation complemented with hard work.

2. Visualise as you relish your favourite food:

How do you savour your favourite platter of dish when served on an empty stomach, you go ballistic right! That's the most important thing of the moment and you wouldn't trade it for anything else. In a similar fashion can you give few minutes unruffled to you visualisation practice as well, 2-3 times a day. While starting you may begin with one session of 5-10 minutes and slowly increase the time up to an hour. In a day, one session can be longer while others can be situational short practices based on the specific goals. You can visualise even under 30 seconds before an important event or for long stretches based on your schedule. It is important to strike a balance between both efforts and visual imagination.

3. Frame personalised phrases of affirmations in present tense and practice as many times as possible:

    If you have difficulty controlling your anger and has resulted in your downfall in some situations you can repeat the following affirmations to change you believe system:

    "krodhād bhavati sammohaḥ sammohāt smṛiti-vibhramaḥ
    smṛiti-bhranśhād buddhi-nāśho buddhi-nāśhāt praṇaśhyati"

    This is a famous Sanskrit shloka from Bhagvad Geeta which means: Anger leads to clouding of judgment, which results in bewilderment of memory. When memory is bewildered, the intellect gets destroyed; and when the intellect is destroyed, one is ruined".
    Similarly, you may create or choose phrases to come out of any other demoralising situation in life. To come out from the state of laziness, you can say something like:

Sleep and Laziness are the biggest enemies of success. When you are met with a failure, you may affirm something like: Failure is the stepping stone to success or Failure is the learning curve needed to improve further etc. Every negative encounter's meaning can be changed by reframing and affirming the right message repeatedly.

Chapter Summary:

1. Follow the Big 4 rule popularised by psychologist Eric Portterat to come out of any difficult situation. A) Focus on the right now. B) Imagine how good it will feel (achievement of the outcome). C) When all fails, Breathe deeply. D)Cheer yourself on

2. Visualisation is an Open Canvas that helps you paint a picture of your liking where you are the main protagonist.

3. Brain cannot differentiate between what is already true and what is fiction and can be tricked into believing the aspirations to be true. Thereby helping develop the mindset and skillset needed to achieve those aspirations.

4. Visualisation is practiced across disciplines and celebrities like Jim Carey and Arnold Schwarzenegger have openly spoken about it reaping the benefits of this method.

5. Visualisation speeds up the learning process and makes you calmer and more resilient.

6. We are mostly following a script handed out to us by others, through visualisation we can think out of the box and create our own destiny

7. Visualisation helps take a pause to think beyond in a world where almost everything is running on autopilot.

8. Most of the time is wasted thinking about the past, thinking what we shouldn't have done, instead of being present in the moment.

9. Visualisation must be done by impressing the events on all five senses of touch, taste, smell, auditory, and sight.

10. Visualisation must be done under the boundary or morality, with a sense of giving first than taking.

11. Affirmations are used to re-program the subconscious mind towards the outlook we desire.

References:

Chapter 1:

1.Angela Duckworth "Grit: The Power of Passion and Perseverance" 2023

2.Nitin Agarwal "India's Greatest Speeches" 2014, p 148-155

Chapter 2:

1.Kate Murphy "You are not listening" Chapter 2 -Listening to opposite views

Chapter 3:

1.Sachin Jha "From Lantern to LIGHTHOUSE" V.K. Bansal journey to the Top

2.https://en.wikipedia.org/wiki/Gukesh_Dommaraju#:~:text=At%20the%20World%20Chess%20Championship,18%20years%20and%20195%20days.

3. Nitin Agarwal "India's Greatest Speeches" 2014, p 98-111

4. Jim Collins, "Good to Great" 2001 p 50

5. Simon Sinek, "Start with why" 2007

6. James Clear, "Atomic Habits" 2018

7. Jim Collins, "Good to Great",2001 p 94-97

8. Norman Vincent Peale "The power of positive thinking" p 87

9. Hector Garcia and Francesco Miralles "Ikigai The Japanese secret to a long and happy life"2016 p 14-15

Chapter 4:

Pavan Joshni "Design your thinking"2022, p 10-15

Chapter 5:

1.Lally, P., Van Jaarsveld, C. H. M., Potts, H. W. W., & Wardle, J. (2010). How are habits formed: Modelling habit formation in the real world. *European Journal of Social Psychology, 40*(6), 998–1009. https://doi.org/10.1002/ejsp.674

2.Stephan MR Covey with Rebecca R Merill "The speed of Trust"2006 p 288-293

Chapter 6:

1.https://en.wikipedia.org/wiki/Dwight_D._Eisenhower

2. https://www.businessinsider.in/research-shows-we-touch-our-cell-phones-2617-times-per-day/articleshow/53197026.cms

3. https://www.cbsnews.com/news/survey-75-percent-of-americans-admit-to-using-phone-while-in-bathroom/

4. https://yougov.co.uk/society/articles/22551-most-britons-use-their-phone-toilet

Chapter 7:

1. https://time.com/3858309/attention-spans-goldfish/

2. https://pib.gov.in/PressReleasePage.aspx?PRID=2043805&ut m_

3. Kahneman, D., & Tversky, A. (1979). Prospect Theory: An Analysis of Decision under Risk. *Econometrica, 47*(2), 263–291. https://doi.org/10.2307/1914185

4. https://growthlist.co/startup-failure-statistics/

Chapter 8:

1.Tom Hoobyar & Tom Dots with Susan Anders NLP The Essential Guide 2013, p-110;

2.Stephan R Covery "The 7 Habits of highly Effective people 1989, p-99;

3.Naplean Hill, "Think and grow rich" 1937.

4.https://www.forbes.com/sites/lidijaglobokar/2020/03/05/the-power-of-visualization-and-how-to-use-it/

5.https://www.researchgate.net/publication/344587632_Visualisation_techniques_in_sport_-_the_mental_road_map_for_success

6. https://medium.com/illumination/only-1-of-linkedin-users-write-content-whats-up-with-the-other-99-48263f86b678

About The Author

Ajay is a motivational speaker, sales and marketing consultant working for a Medtech Company based in Bangalore. After having worked in 3 amongst the top 10 healthcare companies of the world, he started working for technology startups in healthcare domain to learn the intricacies of starting an organization in the healthcare industry. He loves giving motivational talks to organizations looking to boost the morale of their employees and increase productivity. He also has a YouTube Channel by the name of "Leadership Redefined with AJ", where he speaks on the areas of Leadership and management in his free time.

Ajay Lives in Bangalore.